What other experts are saying

"When I first started leading teams, I had little idea what to do. There were so many aspects to leadership that study alone did not equip me to deal with. The one thing I was certain about was my curiosity and need to learn. There was also a need to unlearn what I thought I knew and to have the courage to do so. This new publication by Karen Ferris provides the roadmap of discovery and a way of embracing and relearning the skills to become the best leader today. As leaders, we are dealing with multi-generational teams, and what worked twenty years ago will not work now. So, what are you going to do? Embrace the change and have the humility to ask for help or stay stagnant in your old ways of working? The choice is yours. Your help lies within these pages."

Mary-Beth Hosking MBT
CEO of Vic ICT for Women

"Karen Ferris provides practical, actionable advice for leaders at every level that they can use to cultivate the mindset and characteristics they need to succeed in today's complex and uncertain world. Recognizing that change is the only constant today, she will show you how to adapt and evolve so as to face the challenges and take advantage of the opportunities that tomorrow is sure to bring."

Bryce Hoffman
Bestselling author (*American Icon: Alan Mulally and the Fight to Save Ford Motor Company*), speaker, president of Red Team Thinking

"Karen Ferris is one of those names which will stand the test of time when it comes to looking back to the period and understanding what it was that shaped the landscape of work in the post-pandemic world. There's a need for change and transformation, and the absolute imperative is that leaders comprehend change, not only around them but also within themselves. This is not the first time that Karen dives deep into what it is that makes the essence of good teaming and lowers something I call human debt. She has spent the last twenty-plus years debating it, curating articles about it, studying the work of others, and doing hands-on work with all types of industries with these needs. They all have one thing in common: the imperative of acquiring the resilience, the Emotional Intelligence (EQ), the empathy and the humanizing skills that tech cultures demand. If you want to learn the skills and eliminate your human debt and possibly even tech debt too, you need to read this book, you need to follow its author, and you need to take it to heart."

Duena Blomstrom
Creator of the Human Debt™ concept, author of *People Before Tech* and *Tech-Led Culture*, neurospicy leader in technology, international speaker, podcaster, media personality

"Are you looking for a practical guide to help you navigate the ever-evolving world of work? Look no further than Karen's new book, which provides a human approach to work that is future-focused, effective, and feels good. Using a memorable acronym, Karen's book is a valuable resource for leaders and employees alike. Whether you're a seasoned professional or just starting out, this book will help you develop the mindset you need to succeed in today's fast-paced world. Mindset is everything and leaders at all levels who want to be remarkable will be well served by this thoughtful and practical book. I highly recommend reading and applying Karen's teachings. An ever-evolving workforce and nonstop change means that ongoing learning is the key to success. This book is a great resource for a world of work faced with disruption."

Nola Simon
Hybrid remote futurist, LinkedIn® Top Voice 2024, keynote speaker, podcaster

"Be REMARKABLE! takes a hard look at a soft skill – leadership. Karen Ferris's new book is a detailed toolkit for leadership at all levels. It richly illustrates a path for your leadership journey – plotting practical advice to upgrade key skills, including resilience, empathy, adaptability, listening, and more..."

Gavin McMahon
Co-founder and CEO of fassforward, LinkedIn® Top Thought Leader, storytelling voice, executive coach, keynote speaker

Be REMARKABLE!

Also by Karen Ferris:

Game On! Change is Constant

Unleash the Resiliator Within—Resilience:
A Handbook for Individuals

Unleash the Resiliator Within—Resilience:
A Handbook for Leaders

Balanced Diversity

Be REMARKABLE!

Learn to Unlearn:
The New Leadership Mindset

KAREN FERRIS

To all the rebels who went before and are yet to come.

Thank you, Breed, my beautiful wife and best friend.

Contents

About the author

Karen Ferris is a self-professed organizational change rebel *with a cause*. She will constantly challenge the status quo when her reason for doing so is defensible.

Karen began her life in IT and spent most of that in IT service management (ITSM). She is still recognized as one of the leading experts in that space. For the most part, she was a people leader.

As someone continually focused on the people side of change, she authored a publication titled *Balanced Diversity: A Portfolio Approach to Organizational Change* in 2011 She considered herself an accidental author back then. She stumbled across a framework for embedding change, set out to write a white paper on using it with ITSM, and ended up writing a book. Karen realized she had always been doing organizational change management but never called it that. The book propelled Karen formally into the industry.

In 2019 she authored *Game On! Change is Constant: Tactics to Win When Leading Change Is Everyone's Business* to prepare organizations and everyone in them for constant and uncertain change.

The year 2020 saw the publication of two books: *Unleash the Resiliator Within – Resilience: A Handbook for Individuals* and its companion, *A Handbook for Leaders*. In the same year, Karen revised her *Balanced Diversity* book, making it applicable to any industry.

Born in Liverpool, Karen emigrated to Australia in 1998 and now lives in Melbourne with her wife, Breed. Her consultancy practice focuses on organizational change management, workforce resilience, leadership capability uplift, and remote working. She is a sought-after international keynote speaker and accomplished consultant.

Karen is an avid Liverpool Football Club supporter, an Elvis fan, a calceophile, and an arctophile. You may need to Google those!

Are you willing to unlearn?

It was the American businessman and futurist Alvin Toffler who said, "The illiterate of the 21st century will not be those who cannot read and write, but those who cannot learn, unlearn, and relearn."

He made that prediction in his 1970 book *Future Shock*[1], which explores how rapid change can overwhelm people. Future shock refers to people's physical and psychological distress when they cannot cope with the rapidity of social and technological changes.

An example of future shock is the rapid emergence of artificial intelligence (AI) and applications such as ChatGPT. Launched in November 2022, ChatGPT is a natural language processing tool that allows you to have human-like conversations with a chatbot. It can answer questions and undertake tasks such as writing essays, composing emails, creating apps, building resumes, writing Excel formulas, summarizing content, and writing code.

Many roles were suddenly under threat, including content writers, researchers, data analysts, creative writers, reporters and journalists, lawyers and paralegals, accountants and auditors, teachers, designers, data entry clerks, and customer service agents. Those people had two choices: be a victim or adopt a learning mindset (often called a growth mindset). A growth mindset is the belief that you can develop your skills, competencies, and capacities through effort and commitment.

Those with a learning mindset set out to learn new, unique skills or enhance their existing skills so that artificial intelligence (AI) could not replace them. For example, my friend Bob was an accountant who provided essential services and knew that AI could do most of his daily work. He also realized that there would always be a need for good accountants. Each business that accountants work with is unique, and accountants may often have to provide customized solutions to address specific needs such as financial restructuring or tax planning. He knew this type of problem-solving and solution provision required creativity, adaptability, and an in-depth understanding of the business's needs. These skills were not easily automated.

Bob embarked on becoming a chartered accountant with Chartered Accountants Australia and New Zealand (CA ANZ). He knew he had the level of competency to enter the program and was determined to gain the credential. The learning would enable him to provide the more complex accountancy services businesses require. Bob also knew that if he could learn how to utilize AI to be more effective and efficient in his job, he would have an advantage over accountants who did not. Bob's learning mindset and victor-over-victim mentality were critical to his success. He now manages one of the leading boutique accountancy companies in Australia. This is all because he was willing to *learn, unlearn, and relearn*.

Learn, unlearn, relearn

The hardest part of the learn, unlearn, relearn approach is unlearn. Most people are familiar with learning, but unlearning is often a new concept. It is more than forgetting something you learned some time ago, like how to speak French. It is about making space for new ideas and perspectives. To do that, you must let go of ingrained ways of thinking and operating to make way for relearning.

You must let go of things that may have worked well for you in the past. You must challenge your long-held assumptions and be open to changing your mindset. It is about the courage to change and the humility to admit that what you knew yesterday may no longer be relevant. Unlearning is a process of questioning the validity of what you believe in.

In his 2007 book *What Got You Here Won't Get You There: How Successful People Become Even More Successful!*[2], Marshall Goldsmith (executive leadership coach) identified twenty-one behaviors you must eliminate if you want to be successful. He argued that while these behaviors may not have stopped you from getting "here" – to your current level of success – they won't get you "there" – to the heights of success you ultimately aspire to. To be an effective leader, you must eliminate and replace some learning with new learning.

One of the most recent examples of "unlearn" was a result of the COVID-19 pandemic. Before the pandemic, many managers (note I have not used the term "leader") had an entrenched belief that if they could see their employees at their desks, then those employees were being productive. Now, you and I know that this isn't necessarily the case. However, this engrained delusion drove many other behaviors, such as presenteeism.

Post-pandemic, many employees wanted to maintain the autonomy and flexibility they had experienced while working from home, while many employers were mandating a return to the office. The mandate was a direct response to a need to unlearn. If managers could not see their employees, how would they know they were working? Many managers have time-managed employees for decades. This behavior was going to be hard to unlearn.

These managers now had to learn how to performance manage employees based on outcomes, not hours at a desk. They needed to provide clear goals and trust their employees to deliver. They had to change how they rewarded their employees. No longer were employees rewarded for working twelve-hour days. Managers (the good ones, at least) now reward employees for the value they deliver.

I have worked with many leadership teams through workshops and one-on-one coaching sessions to enable them to (a) realize the need to unlearn and (b) assist them in relearning how to manage performance effectively regardless of employee location. Unlearning is the biggest challenge as most people have been used to "acquisitive" learning, which is adding more learning and acquiring new knowledge on top of what was already there. Unlearning means continually questioning and challenging your knowledge to ensure it is relevant and current.

As Chinese philosopher Lao Tzu said, "To attain knowledge, add things every day. To attain wisdom, remove things every day."

To unlearn, you need to:

1. Recognize and accept that the knowledge that has worked so far is no longer relevant or has limited value. The sooner you recognize this, the sooner you can move in a new

direction. Seek feedback on your beliefs, behaviors, and modus operandi to help determine their relevancy.

2. Learn to unlearn and seek the opportunity to relearn. You will replace the knowledge you eliminate with new knowledge. Being open-minded, curious, and intentional helps you unlearn. Focus on the latest knowledge and break your old patterns of thought and behavior.

3. Remain open to new experiences and knowledge. Do not unlearn and relearn only to close the door again. Continually question and challenge what you know, and ensure it is relevant and current. Keep learning to unlearn and relearn. As in step one, keep seeking feedback and adjust as needed.

As Adam Grant (psychologist, professor, and author) said on X, "It takes curiosity to learn. It takes courage to unlearn. Learning requires the humility to admit what you don't know today. Unlearning requires the integrity to admit that you were wrong yesterday. Learning is how you evolve. Unlearning is how you keep up as the world evolves."[3]

Of course, this will not be possible overnight. Mastering the concept of unlearning will take time, practice, and the right mindset. That's the focus of this book.

This book is your compass

In a world constantly in flux, with unforeseen challenges shaping the landscape of business and society, traditional leadership skills are no longer the sole reason for success. Leadership today is as much about mindset as it is about skill sets. It is about cultivating a learning mindset that embraces constant change and can adapt. This book is an odyssey through the landscape of leadership mindsets, proposing a transformative approach that stands robust against the seismic shifts of our time.

I delve into the crucible of effective leadership, advocating for a mindset that is not just equipped but also agile, and open to unlearning and relearning in the face of rapid and disruptive change. The ability to engage in difficult conversations, make tough decisions, remain self-aware, resourceful, and courageous, and be both empowering and empathetic is not merely advantageous but essential.

Leadership transcends the confines of acquired skills – it demands a psychological shift. It is the shift to a learning mindset, recognizing that yesterday's knowledge may not necessarily resolve today's challenges. The advent of disruptive technologies like artificial intelligence, with tools such as the aforementioned ChatGPT, as well as Claude, Google Gemini, and Microsoft Bing, has thrust upon us an imperative to adapt or become redundant. The choices you make, to fall prey to technological incursion or to rise above it through continuous learning and relearning, define your trajectory in this new era.

This book charts the concept of unlearning, a concept less traversed but equally vital. Unlearning is about creating intellectual and emotional space for new ideas, questioning long-held assumptions, and being open to change. It is the humility to accept that yesterday's solutions may not answer tomorrow's questions. I draw on real-world examples to illustrate the perils of not unlearning and the rewards of relearning.

This book is not just a narrative but a toolkit. It will guide you through the individual elements of the REMARKABLE mindset, offering insights into developing each facet to its full potential. From being resilient in the maelstrom of change to embodying empathy, from practicing mindfulness to being adaptive, from showing resourcefulness to establishing your unique leadership brand, each aspect is meticulously unpacked and explored.

Whether you're an emerging leader or a seasoned executive, this book offers a transformative lens through which to view your role and gives you the courage to reshape it. Join me on this journey to unlock the REMARKABLE leadership mindset within you, navigate the labyrinth of leadership challenges with grace, and emerge triumphant. The future belongs to those prepared to learn, unlearn, and relearn; this book is your compass.

The REMARKABLE leader

Before we embark on this journey together, allow me to share some more information about myself and the REMARKABLE leadership mindset.

For over twenty years, I have delivered consultancy services to large, medium, and small organizations in many industry sectors. My consultancy business delivers value to organizations in three core areas: organizational change management, workforce resilience, and leadership capability uplift. I have leveraged my extensive experience in these fields in writing this book, enabling you to become a remarkable leader.

The book was inspired by my observation of many leaders, from novice to veteran, who firmly believed that what stood them in good stead as leaders yesterday would continue to do so tomorrow. There was a dangerous lack of comprehension that when the world around you changes, you must change too. Otherwise, you become irrelevant.

This was more prevalent in leaders who experienced success. Their success at the time undid their future success because their success made them cautious. When you have nothing to lose, you are prepared to change. When you have something to lose, you are reluctant. However, you must have the ability to continually adapt and evolve to thrive in new circumstances, remain relevant, and deliver value.

Be REMARKABLE! – Learn to Unlearn: The New Leadership Mindset comprehensively examines the intrinsic qualities of effective leadership in today's volatile world. The acronym "REMARKABLE" encapsulates the leader who is: **Resilient, Empathetic, Mindful, Adaptive, Resourceful, Known, Accountable, Brave, Listening,** and **Empowering.**

Figure 1: The REMARKABLE leadership mindset

© 2024 Karen Ferris

This table provides a summary of each mindset element.

	Resilient	The leader is resilient in the face of constant and disruptive change. They have a positive outlook and see setbacks as learning opportunities.
	Empathetic	Empathy is a genuine interest and concern for team members and employees of the organization. The leader understands individual needs, values, aspirations, challenges, and concerns. They provide leadership and support.
	Mindful	The leader practices self-awareness, self-regulation, and emotional control. They are a humble leader.
	Adaptive	The adaptive leader embraces change, challenges the status quo, experiments, and innovates. They identify technical and adaptive problems, and tackle the latter with dynamic, people-focused solutions.
	Resourceful	Resourcefulness means a focus on what matters. The leader categorizes, prioritizes, and delegates. They focus on getting the right things done at the right time by the right person.
	Known	The leader possesses a clear and unique leadership brand. They live their stated values. They have defined what they want to be known for.
	Accountable	Goals are communicated and aligned. The leader owns their commitments and promises. They are answerable to the actions and decisions they make and those made by the team.

	Brave	The leader dares to be vulnerable and admit their mistakes. They are prepared to have the hard conversations and make the hard decisions. They are ready to unlearn and step outside of their comfort zone.
	Listening	The listening mindset means the leader is an effective communicator and an active listener. They are present, attentive, and remain in the moment. They ensure understanding.
	Empowering	The leader has moved away from a command and control approach to one of empowerment and trust. They provide clarity of goals and expectations and then get out of the way.

Each section of the book is dedicated to one of these attributes, unpacking its relevance and application in the context of modern challenges – from the rise of artificial intelligence to the aftermath of global crises like the COVID-19 pandemic. There's also an additional section, up next, exploring the different stages of the leader's journey. The book provides not only theoretical essentials, but also practical advice drawn from real-world examples and the latest research on leadership and organizational behavior.

Whether you are an emerging leader or a seasoned executive, this book will guide you in honing a leadership mindset attuned to the nuances of an ever-evolving landscape. Prepare to transform your approach to leadership and foster a culture of continuous learning and growth.

The leader's journey

The process of learning-unlearning-relearning is a journey you will embark on. I liken your leadership journey to the hero's journey.

The hero's journey is a classic story structure derived from Joseph Campbell's monomyth from his book *The Hero with a Thousand Faces*.[4] The hero goes on a quest to achieve a goal and must overcome obstacles and fears before embarking on the return journey home.

There are three stages to the hero's journey:

- Separation: the hero leaves the familiar world behind
- Initiation: the hero learns to navigate the unfamiliar world
- Return: the hero returns to the familiar world

Many movies follow the hero's journey, including *Star Wars*, *The Matrix*, *The Wizard of Oz*, *The Goonies*, and many Disney classics. In each film, the hero leaves the world they are familiar with and enters a new one. They go on an adventure, learn lessons, claim a victory, and, with their newfound knowledge, return home transformed.

Your journey will not be one in which you join the Rebel Alliance against the Galactic Empire, fight powerful computers, melt the Wicked Witch of the West, or search for a legendary pirate's long-lost treasure. But I promise you it will be epic. Having recognized the need for change, you will leave your comfort zone, unlearn and relearn, and return with a leadership mindset that makes you REMARKABLE.

This is the leader's journey.

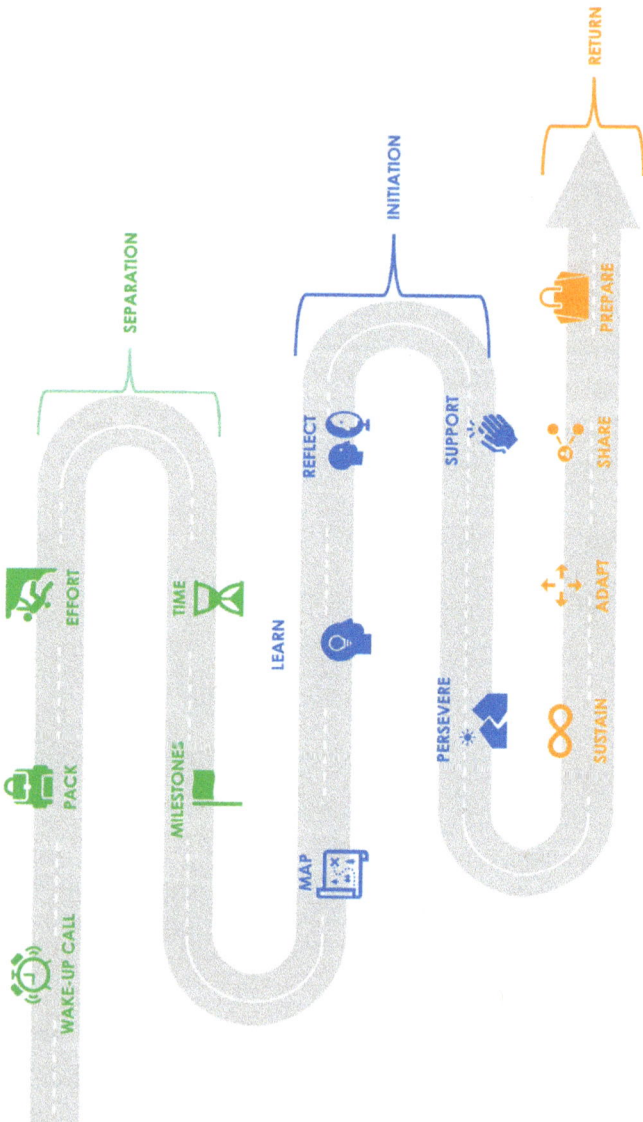

Figure 2: The leader's journey

Separation

To embark on the journey, you must not only know you need to change but have recognized the hindrance your current behaviors are to your success and that of your teams and the organization. You acknowledge that your current learnings no longer serve you and that you must unlearn and relearn.

Many events could lead to this recognition. It could be feedback from colleagues or team members. It could be a light bulb moment – the wake-up call.

Figure 3: The leader's journey – separation

Wake-up call

I have seen that wake-up call happen when I run leadership workshops on empowerment and accountability. When I talk about employee empowerment to leaders who have always led from the front and made the decisions, I see the rabbit caught in the headlights. They receive the word "empowerment" but hear "erosion." They receive the word "autonomy" but hear "anarchy."

I suggest they select a small and low-risk task with which they could empower a trusted employee and allow them the autonomy to undertake the task as they see fit, and I ask, "What is the worst thing that could happen?" When I suggest they try it and prepare for the overwhelming difference it makes in engagement and motivation, I can see the lights going on.

They experience the difference and receive the wake-up call to change. The journey begins. They have the ah-ha moment about how much time they have freed up. There is the realization that this is a journey, and there is no expectation that they will move from a position of command and control to empowerment and trust overnight. They will be given the support to embark on the journey.

Pack

You must pack for your journey intentionally. By that I mean, be prepared. Accept that there will be twists and turns, setbacks and delays, wrong turns, and obstacles to overcome. Be honest with yourself, acknowledging your strengths and weaknesses. Do not start on the journey unless you are genuinely committed to it and prepared to make a concerted effort.

When working to uplift leadership capability, I tell my participants to "Pack a good dose of self-awareness." They must know and understand the things that make them who they are. Research shows a strong link between self-awareness and high performance in leaders. When you are aware of your strengths and weaknesses, you have the power to build on the strengths and eliminate the weaknesses.

As Dr Phil (television host and author) said, "You cannot change what you do not acknowledge."[5]

Effort

It is imperative from the outset that you acknowledge the commitment and effort required to change your leadership style genuinely. Don't underestimate it. You will need resilience to keep moving when the going gets tough, and it likely will. There will be doubts, fears, uncertainty, and wavering.

Time

You must be patient and recognize the time it will take to adjust your leadership style. Not managing your expectations can thwart the journey from the outset. I have worked with leaders who look for a shortcut. "Just tell me what to do," they say. Well, it doesn't work like that. Take the critical skill of empathy. I can help people develop the capacity and capability to be empathetic through self-awareness, questioning, and listening. But you cannot just *do* empathy. You must *feel* empathy. It is about understanding and sharing the feelings of another. It cannot be forced, and it can take time.

Milestones

You must recognize the milestones you achieve on your journey. The end goal can be daunting as it is so far away, so identifying the small achievements provides encouragement and motivation. The milestones could be a small step forward, a comeback, and learning from a setback. All are worthy of celebration. Setbacks present a learning opportunity and, therefore, should be lauded. Recognizing milestones can make a seemingly long and arduous journey feel more manageable.

When I work with leaders on skills such as empowerment, I ask them to identify their milestones before they leave the learning environment to utilize their learning back in the workplace. Often, the milestones are forgotten with the enthusiasm to just get on with the journey. Milestones are important to pause and reflect on. When you appreciate the accomplishment of the smaller steps, you are motivated to accomplish the bigger ones. Milestones for empowerment could be the first task delegated, and empowerment and autonomy enabled. The second could be a more significant task. The next one could be a group task, and so on.

Initiation

Initiation is making the transition to a new leadership mindset. This is where our hero crosses the point of no return and undergoes transformative stages. Here, you must practice everything you learn on your journey to overcome the obstacle that forms the story's climax.

Figure 4: The leader's journey – initiation

Map

You must map out your journey. What are the skills you need to develop or improve? How will you do that? Where will you do it?

Think about your strengths and where they work well. Do they work well in many situations? For example, you may have excellent interpersonal skills with your team – with people you have known for some time and established a level of trust with. You may find it challenging to leverage those interpersonal skills with another area of the organization with which you have no relationship.

You may be great at encouraging collaboration across a network of people over whom you have no management responsibility. They see you as a coach rather than a manager. With your team, to whom you have management responsibility, this may be a challenge as your encouragement of collaboration is seen as more of an instruction. The challenge is how to develop that skill with your team.

You must also map out how you will get feedback on your skills when you utilize them in various situations.

I encourage leaders to make a map of their learning journey so they can set realistic learning goals with timeframes and visualize the journey. There is no one-size-fits-all approach to creating a learning map as everyone is different. However, there are some basic things to include for each learning:

- Which skill do you want to develop (the topic)?
- What do you want to achieve from this learning (the goal)?
- How are you going to learn (the context/s)?
- What is your timeframe (the target date)?

These constructs will be repeated for each skill to be developed. You can also update your learning map as your priorities change or you determine additional contexts to include.

Learn

There are many methods and tools you can use to facilitate your learning. The choice of learning approach will be influenced by the strength you are developing and the most effective way to practice it. Here are some suggestions:

- **Formal training** focuses on developing your identified needs. It could be classroom-based, virtual, or a blended option. It could be in real-time or on-demand.
- **Action and experiential learning** enables you to learn by doing. This learning provides direct experience and focused reflection. It immerses you in real-world challenges. These could be direct work experiences

such as leading a new cross-functional team. It could be business simulation exercises where you are engaged in new experiences in a safe environment without risk.

- **Technology and e-learning platforms** are used for development programs, which could include webinars, seminars, and interactive platforms.
- **Coaching and mentoring** give you access to experienced people who can provide guidance and support. These individuals can foster personalized development and help you navigate challenges.

Learning and development can also be achieved by attending conferences, networking events, and forums. Reading periodicals, newsletters, industry publications, and social media can increase the learning capacity.

You must practice your new skills, and you must determine the best context in which to do this. It could be beneficial to practice on a team to whom you are unknown as a leader, or the opposite could apply.

Reflect

It is essential that you regularly reflect on your progress. This is a time when you can celebrate small wins but also celebrate the setbacks as learning opportunities. You must consider how far you have come and not lose sight of the end game.

When you can only see the end game, it can create feelings of despair as it seems so far away and unachievable. Remember that it is an end game and does not have to happen immediately. The end game is where you are heading and should fill you with possibility and passion. It should not frustrate you, as you can see your progress toward it. You are moving along the path to make it happen.

So, reflect on the end game and the steps to get there. Reflect on how far you have come and how much you have achieved. Celebrate. You deserve it!

Support

Do not do this on your own. You need a support team who will cheer you on, provide encouragement and motivation, and keep you on the hook to achieve your goals. They will give honest feedback and draw your attention to unacceptable actions or behaviors. Your support team can consist of coaches, mentors, and trusted colleagues. You must ensure that people feel safe to provide you with feedback, so you must create an environment of psychological safety.

You can encourage a broader audience to provide feedback by letting people know you are on a journey to improve your leadership. When you share this information and dare to be vulnerable, you show people you care. As a result, people will help and support you, especially when you have a setback.

It is imperative that you thank people for their feedback and encourage more. You must act on the feedback you receive. If you don't, people will stop providing the vital feedback you need to improve your leadership skills.

You must proactively seek regular feedback regarding your performance as a leader. The critical thing is to remember that feedback is generally not personal. It is not about you as a person but about you as a leader and how well you perform in that role.

When a person is brave enough to give you unfavorable feedback, your duty as the leader is to take it on board and own it. While you may feel upset, angry, or disappointed by what you hear, you must see this as an opportunity for improvement, growth, and development. Just as positive feedback is an opportunity to do more of the same, negative feedback is an opportunity to do things differently.

Persevere

Resist the urge to return to your familiar territory – your comfort zone. It is important to remember that each time you step outside your comfort zone, your comfort zone gets bigger. Your comfort zone is your safe place. It is where you feel in control.

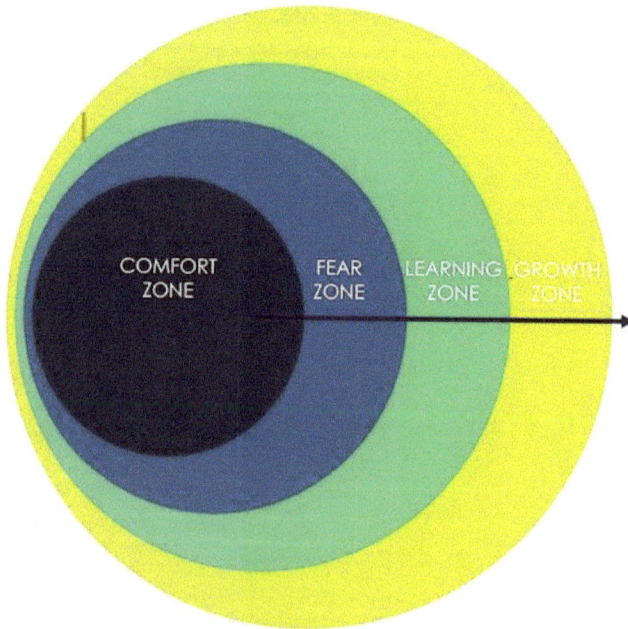

Figure 5: The learning and growth zones

You will need to find the courage to step into the fear zone. This is why you need your map. You can build on previous experiences. In the fear zone, you may look for excuses to return to your comfort zone. Don't. Persevere! When you persevere, you will enter the learning zone where you will develop the leadership skills you need. This is where you are extending your comfort zone.

After a period of learning, you will have created a new comfort zone, increasing your ability to reach new levels of leadership. This is what it means to be in the growth zone, where you can set new goals.

Return

You embark on the return part of the journey after the challenges of a somewhat long and arduous voyage. The learnings are now embedded, and a more empowering leadership style emerges that can be utilized widely. Learning does not end here. You must sustain it.

Figure 6: The leader's journey – return

Sustain

This is where you sustain your learning by doing. It is the persistent, self-initiated pursuit of excellence in leadership. You must keep applying your learning in different contexts to retain it long term. Sustained learning helps you think and behave in new ways.

Consistent and conscious practice over time forms new behaviors and ways of thinking. Neuro-scientifically speaking, you create new neural connections and pathways (also known as "neuroplasticity"). Through repetition and practice, these neural patterns overtake old ones so you can think and behave in new ways.

Continue to solicit feedback on your performance and act upon it.

Adapt

When applying your learning, you also need to be able to adapt your leadership style. You need to know when to direct and when to provide direction (yes, there is a difference). You will face situations where a more directive leadership style will be called upon. You must make that judgment. The good news is that you now have a portfolio of leadership skills.

With a directive style, you are typically the person who defines the solution and then tells the team or individual what to do. With a non-directive style, you help the team or individual arrive at the solution themselves, usually by asking guiding questions. You empower them to do so.

Directive and non-directive leadership could be described as "push" and "pull" techniques. Each will bring about different outcomes. If you want people to comply and get fast results, you will choose "push." Suppose you want commitment and changes in behavior. If you want to empower people to solve problems themselves and be more self-sufficient for the future, you will choose "pull." "Pull" takes longer but has a long-term impact. Pull techniques also tend to be more effective in persuasion and overcoming resistance, and can help stimulate critical thinking.

You would use a directive leadership style if you are in an office during a fire, for example. You would decide the solution – get out of the building – and tell (direct) your employees what you want them to do. You would *not* be a non-directive leader and encourage employees to decide what to do for themselves.

Share

Now that you are in the return stage, you can share what you have learned with others. You can use it to develop others. Here's an example.

In your team meetings, you have become acutely aware of a lack of questioning within discussions. You talk to some trusted team members and uncover a fear of reprimand or repercussion if decisions are challenged. You learned on your journey that for people to give feedback openly and honestly, there must be an environment of psychological safety. As a result, you strive to ensure everyone in the team feels safe to voice their thoughts and take risks. You then share your proven approach with other leaders in the organization.

Prepare

The journey is never over. Looking back over the last two decades, the nature of leadership expected in successful organizations has shifted from an autocratic style toward a more collaborative approach, fostering greater teamwork, productivity, innovation, and creativity. What will be the required or preferred leadership style in another twenty years? Many predictions are floating around.

As it stands, leaders need to be agile, highly entrepreneurial, socially conscious, and digitally savvy. They must navigate through ambiguity and uncertainty, often while managing a diverse workforce.

The world is changing so fast that in twenty years, leaders will most likely need different skills and competencies than the ones they're expected to have today. You must start to prepare for that learning journey now. Get ready to unlearn and relearn – and become a REMARKABLE leader in the process.

Resilient, Part 1

According to the American Psychological Association (APA), "Resilience is the process and outcome of successfully adapting to difficult or challenging life experiences, especially through mental, emotional, and behavioral flexibility and adjustment to external and internal demands."[6]

Many variations of that definition exist, and a high proportion use the terminology "bounce back from setbacks." I prefer to use the term "bounce forward." When you *bounce forward*, you learn from the experience and are better for it. You are more resilient as a result. Setbacks inform you and help you do things differently the next time. They are opportunities to learn, develop, and grow.

A resilient mindset enables you to:

- Accept ambiguity and embrace uncertainty
- Act thoughtfully
- Manage your emotions
- Be self-aware
- Maintain a positive outlook
- Connect, collaborate, and build networks
- Operate with empathy
- Maintain a growth mindset
- Be confident in your abilities and make good use of your strengths

The benefits to you and your team in being resilient include:

- Better physical and mental health

- Improved cognitive functioning
- Maintaining inner calm in stressful situations
- Seeing life as a series of challenges, not problems
- Stability in the face of a crisis
- Capacity to thrive in conditions of high demand and ongoing pressure
- Ability to recover quickly from setbacks
- Embracing failures and setbacks as learning opportunities
- Reduced burnout
- Increased sense of community

Individual superpowers to build resilience

Back in 2020, I published two books on resilience. I identified twenty superpowers for individuals and twenty for leaders to be resilient in the face of constant, disruptive, uncertain, and complex change. I share all forty superpowers with you in this section (Resilient, Part 1) and the next (Resilient, Part 2).

Resilience is about maintaining your mental well-being, and, unlike many other resources designed to help improve your resilience, these superpowers are contextual. You choose the one or two you need at a particular time based on your challenge or problem. After all, not everyone can overcome a challenge or problem with a mindfulness session!

The following is a summary of the twenty superpowers for you as an individual. For more information on each superpower and how to acquire it, refer to the book *Unleash the Resiliator Within – Resilience: A Handbook for Individuals*.[7]

The Regulator
Stress tolerance and impulse control

The Solver
Effective problem solving

The Realistic Optimist
Belief in change for the better

The Futurist
Long-term perspective

The Empathizer
Awareness of others' feelings, needs and concerns

The Categorizer
Prioritization and focus

The Adapter
Adaptation to change and uncertainty

The Thanker
Gratitude

The Collaborator
Working with others towards shared goals

The Observer
Self-observation

The Achiever
Sense of purpose

The Revealer
Authentic self

The Explorer
Learning, passion and perseverance

The Questioner
Challenge the status quo

The Celebrant
Celebration of success and failure

The Reframer
Change perspective

The Experimenter
Innovation fueled by experimentation

The Believer
Self-belief

The Humorist
Humor as a coping mechanism

The Listener
Effective listening

Figure 7: Individual superpowers

The Regulator

As The Regulator, you can regulate your emotions. You exercise stress tolerance and impulse control. You avoid turning a drama into a crisis and respond to situations rather than react to them. You don't allow your thoughts to cloud your judgment. You pause and reflect to increase your self-awareness. You take time and make the effort to discover yourself and become kind enough to accept your entire self. You exercise emotional intelligence.

Daniel Goleman, an American psychologist, brought emotional intelligence to the forefront in his 1995 book *Emotional Intelligence: Why It Can Matter More Than IQ.*[8] Emotional intelligence is the ability to recognize and understand your emotions while also being able to recognize, understand, and influence the emotions of others. Emotional intelligence helps you build relationships, reduce stress, defuse conflict, and improve job satisfaction.

The Regulator utilizes two of the emotional intelligence dimensions: self-awareness and self-regulation. Self-awareness is knowing what you are feeling and why you are feeling it. It is the cornerstone of emotional intelligence. Self-regulation is intentionally choosing how to respond to those emotions. You increase your resilience when you are aware of your emotions and can control your responses.

To acquire this superpower, I encourage you to gather strategies for stress tolerance and impulse control. I worked with a leader who recognized (self-awareness) that he was impatient and could lose his cool when his team did not deliver as quickly as he wanted. He responded harshly to unfinished tasks and didn't appreciate the completed ones. Having recognized his impatience, he put in place a practice to respond rather than react (self-regulation). When he felt his impatience rising, he would press his thumb against his index finger. When he put that space between the stimulus and the potential reaction, he enabled a better response for himself and the team.

You can also label your emotions, which helps to recognize and regulate them. I coached a young consultant called Mary, who was experiencing bouts of severe anxiety. We worked together to recognize and label the emotion. Labeling allows you to see your thoughts and feelings for what they are: transient data sources that may or may not prove helpful. We worked on self-awareness and asked, "Where, when, who, why?" We labeled the emotion "CIO." It was apparent that when Mary was scheduled to attend a meeting where the CIO was present, her levels of anxiety increased. The CIO was abrasive and rude. We worked on self-management and being able to respond rather than react. Mary would practice breathing exercises before a meeting, knowing that the problem in the meeting was the CIO and not her. She shifted her mindset from being a victim to being a player – that is, someone with intention who would not be manipulated by external factors outside her control.

The Empathizer

The Empathizer understands others' feelings, needs, and concerns. When you develop this superpower, you are attentive to the emotional cues of others and actively listen to what they say. You show sensitivity and understanding of the other person's perspectives. Your behavior is based on understanding the other person's needs and feelings.

Despite extensive research informing us of the benefits of empathetic leaders, such as increased efficiency, creativity, job satisfaction, idea sharing, innovation, and company revenue, it is woefully missing in many organizations.[9] Many employees perceive corporate attempts at empathy as inauthentic. When leaders appear dishonest in their attempts at empathy and don't fulfill promises to employees, trust erodes. In other words, trust breaks down when empathy is simply lip service with no substance. That is just theater.

To become The Empathizer, you must understand what empathy is: the ability to recognize and understand what others are feeling, and understand the underlying reasons for another person's behavior. It is not sympathy. Sympathy is more one-directional – you feel sad for what someone else is experiencing but you may have little comprehension of what that feels like.

Many believe empathy is walking a mile in someone else's shoes. I don't think that describes empathy. Empathy is understanding how the other person feels walking in their shoes. Some would say that compassion comprises empathy – the ability to understand and experience others' emotions – and an intention to benefit others. While empathy is "to feel with someone," compassion is "to be there to help."

Empathy is critical to emotional intelligence, but it is more than recognizing and understanding another person's feelings. It also involves your response based on the information you have collated. Empathy only works effectively where people feel safe expressing themselves without fear of judgment or negative consequences. This is why psychological safety is so important in the workplace. Psychological safety encourages safe and effective interpersonal risk-taking. More on this later.

Not only are empathetic people good communicators, they are also skilled at active listening. They give the other person their undivided attention. They avoid distractions at all costs. They do not interrupt or judge. They remove all biases, filters, and assumptions. They let the other person finish what they have to say. They acknowledge that they are listening. They observe body language, make eye contact, and listen for tonal inflections to understand the underlying meaning of what someone says. We'll discuss this in more detail in the section titled "Listening."

The Collaborator

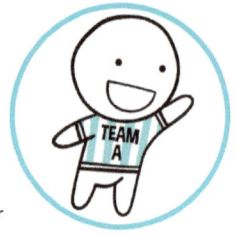

The Collaborator intentionally connects two individuals or a group to work toward achieving a common goal by sharing their ideas and skills. It can happen in co-located or geographically dispersed teams through collaboration tools and platforms. Collaboration means shared learning, breaking down of silos, better problem-solving, and being able to see the bigger picture.

When you are The Collaborator, you are authentic. There is no hidden agenda. You must unite people to work on solutions for the organization's benefit. When tensions between different people or groups emerge, you don't let it become personal; you work to resolve conflict.

You can encourage collaboration by contacting a diverse group and inviting them to connect. Get everyone on the same page. Discuss and agree on the short- and long-term goals, and how you intend to collaborate to achieve them.

Determine which team structure will work best. Ensure you have diversity within the team. Find people with different perspectives and opinions. Select people with the skills and expertise necessary to address the problem to be solved or the opportunity. Include people who are prepared to challenge assumptions and the status quo.

Have clear roles and responsibilities across the group and agree to them. You may want to consider the appointment of a facilitator for the collaboration to keep things focused on the task at hand. However, note that this person is not necessarily the "lead." Give everyone a chance to lead.

Determine the existing collaboration platforms and see if you can leverage them. If no platform exists, determine other tools at your disposal and see if they can help. Investigate available collaboration tools and make a business case for the one that suits your collaboration needs and those of the broader organization. If it is to be an organization-wide platform, this will involve other stakeholder groups.

Make sure everyone understands the behaviors needed to collaborate effectively. Agree on the behaviors and permit everyone to call out any behavior that is not positively contributing to the collaboration. Determine the most appropriate way to celebrate collaboration wins. Do this regularly but not so much that the celebration loses its luster.

The Explorer

The Explorer is curious and inquisitive. Exploration means you are always seeking new challenges and opportunities, and are ready to navigate the uncertain, complex, and disruptive world of change while seeking opportunities for learning, sharing, and growth.

Exploration means asking questions, getting as much information as possible, looking in new places, and finding answers. The Explorer is passionate about learning and will persevere to achieve their goals.

As The Explorer, you will have a **growth mindset** (an idea we'll discuss later in the book) and see a challenge as an opportunity to learn rather than a hurdle or threat to overcome. You will also have **grit**, meaning you can dig deep when the going gets tough. You will have the drive to ignite your passion and sustain your motivation for a long-term goal.

University of Pennsylvania psychologist Angela Duckworth has researched grit's short- and long-term effects on students and people at work. Her research revealed four psychological assets those with grit possess:

- Interest is about enjoying what you do. We all have aspects of our work that we don't enjoy. When you have grit, you can see your work as a whole of many parts, and find it meaningful and exciting.

- Practice is about perseverance and the daily self-control to do something better than you did yesterday. With grit, you strive for mastery through regular and sustained practice. You identify your areas of weakness and work to improve them. There is no room for complacency.

- **Purpose** is what matures passion. Purpose is the belief that your work matters not just for you but for others. Without a purpose, any interest will be difficult to sustain.

- **Hope** enables you to keep going and, if necessary, face your doubts and demons. You might get knocked down, but hope will prompt you to get back up.

The Experimenter

The Experimenter tries new things. It's about being adventurous, embracing the vulnerability that this brings, accepting that there will be mistakes, and recovering from them.

Innovation is now vital to organizational survival, and is fueled by experimentation. You cannot improve things if you are not prepared to experiment. Be prepared for setbacks along the way. Setbacks are a way of learning what doesn't work and what does. If you see setbacks as failures, you will lack resilience.

There are endless stories of innovation failures from successful organizations and people. They are successful because they were prepared to experiment. Examples of failure include Apple III, Google Wave, and Microsoft Zune, yet these organizations thrive. Similarly, 3M Company experimented with glue, which was a failure because it didn't stick (quite literally), but that failure led to the basis for the sticky note, which was a huge success.

If you want to experiment, look at things from a different perspective. Take a walk in someone else's shoes. It could be a customer, consumer, or colleague. Look at how you can improve their experience.

Have a look around and identify things that feel broken. How could you fix them? What could you change? Share thoughts with others and gather their feedback. These findings could lead to different and better ideas.

Extend your view of the world and gather ideas through reading, browsing the internet, and looking at sources of information you wouldn't usually reference.

The Solver

The ability to solve problems effectively is critical to being resilient. How you consider and approach problems helps you build resilience. There are many approaches to problem-solving. The Solver primarily leverages basic problem-solving, creative problem-solving, and design thinking. Here's a quick overview:

Basic problem-solving

1. Define the problem. What issue is it causing?
2. Generate as many solutions as possible.
3. Evaluate all options.
4. Implement a solution and monitor the results to see if it resolves the problem. If it doesn't, return to Step 1.

Creative problem-solving

Creative problem-solving (CPS) is a process formulated by Alex Osborn and Sidney Parnes in the mid-twentieth century. The Creative Education Foundation[10] has a four-stage CPS model with six explicit process steps. Each step uses divergent and convergent thinking. It is called the CPS Learner's Model.[11]

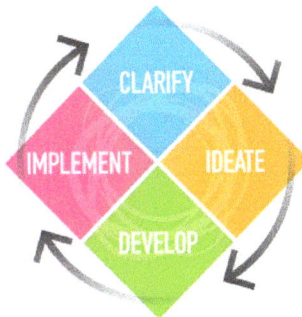

Figure 8: The four-stage CPS model
Learner's Model based on the work of G.J. Puccio, M. Mance, M.C. Murdock,
B. Miller, J. Vehar, R. Firestien, S. Thurber, & D. Nielsen (2011)

Stage	Step	Purpose
CLARIFY	Explore the vision	Identify the goal, wish, or challenge.
	Gather data	Describe and generate data to enable a clear understanding of the challenge.
	Formulate challenges	Sharpen awareness of the challenge and create challenge questions that invite solutions.
IDEATE	Explore ideas	Generate ideas that answer the challenge questions.
DEVELOP	Formulate solutions	To move from ideas to solutions, evaluate, strengthen, and select solutions for the best fit.
IMPLEMENT	Formulate a plan	Explore acceptance, and identify resources and actions that will support the implementation of the selected solution(s).

Design thinking

Design thinking is another approach to creative problem-solving. It is a solution-based approach that uses analytical, synthetic, divergent, and convergent thinking to create many potential solutions, from which you can choose the best fit.

There are many versions of design thinking in use today. I will focus on the five-phase model proposed by the Hasso Plattner Institute of Design at Stanford University, also known as d.school.[12] I have chosen d.school's approach because it's at the forefront of applying and teaching design thinking.

According to d.school, there are five phases of design thinking: empathize, define, ideate, prototype, and test.

DESIGN THINKING PROCESS

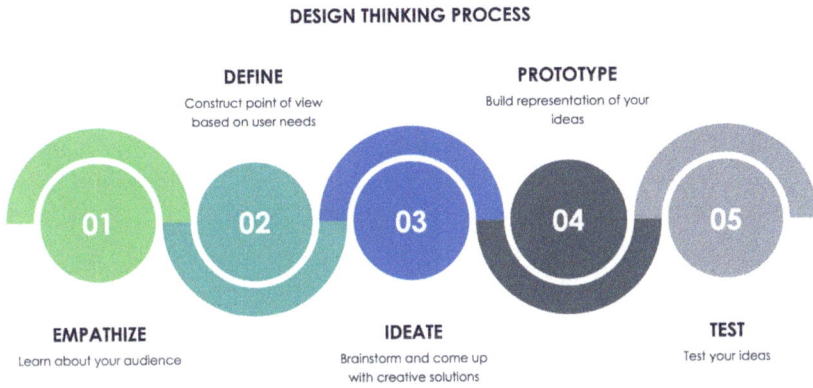

Figure 9: Design thinking process

The Categorizer

The Categorizer uses categorization and compartmentalization to enable focus and build resilience.

If you cannot categorize and compartmentalize, you will not be resilient in the face of constant change. Instead, you will be continually distracted and stressed. You will be thinking of the emails you need to answer while also planning the next team meeting, the next project meeting, and the subsequent report you must write. You will do none of them effectively as each is distracting from the other.

When you categorize work, you focus on one thing at a time. Think of your mind as a set of folders. You must put each task into its corresponding folder. Prioritize the work and pull out the appropriate folder when dealing with it. The art of categorization is even more critical now that we are connected 24/7. Work life can interfere with home life and vice versa. Categorization and prioritization are essential to avoid either life suffering.

I recognize that you may categorize your work and allocate a particular time to "writing that report." Then, despite best intentions, that time gets interrupted by a colleague who wants to pick your brain. You can choose how to deal with the interruption. You can arrange to have the conversation later or accept the interruption, as you think it will only take a few minutes. There is no right or wrong approach. It is what works best for you. But you do need to avoid constant interruption. So, when focusing on one of your work categories, find a place where you are less likely to be disturbed. You could also allocate time to the category of "collaboration" when your door is open for a period, and people know they can come to pick your brain during this time.

Also, when categorizing your work, ask yourself if each category is something you should be doing. The first step to effective categorization is eliminating the work you shouldn't be doing and determining who *should* do it. One of the ways I eliminate or delegate work is to use the action priority matrix. It uses an impact and effort concept. I place the tasks into one of four quadrants:

Quadrant 1: High impact, low effort. These are the quick wins that I will focus on.

Quadrant 2: High impact, high effort. These will require my time but will deliver great value.

Quadrant 3: Low impact, low effort. These are tasks I will delegate.

Quadrant 4: Low impact, high effort. These are tasks I will eliminate.

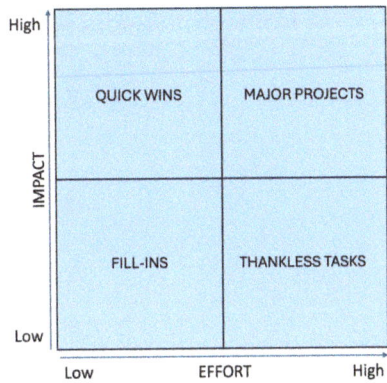

Figure 10: Action priority matrix

It is okay if you can't complete one category in a one-time allocation. Split it into manageable chunks so you have time to complete it. When there's a deadline, whether self-imposed or not, work back from that deadline and allocate time to work on that category. We discuss categorization and prioritization in more detail in "Resourceful."

The Observer

The Observer practices self-observation and mindfulness.

Self-observation, which is the practice of becoming self-aware, is vital to mental well-being and increasing resilience. To grow and become more resilient, you must be able to self-observe. You must regularly look at what you do and how you do it. When you practice self-observation, you are non-judgmental and turn your attention inward to watch your behaviors, words, emotions, and attitudes. Imagine watching yourself from a distance as a character in a movie.

By checking in on yourself, you can make changes that allow you to be more purposeful and effective. Breathing and focus are crucial to self-observation because they help direct inward attention and quiet the mind. When you pay attention to your breathing – slowly inhaling and exhaling – your mental state improves. As your breathing deepens, you will feel grounded. It is essential to gently return focus to your breathing when you notice you have become distracted.

Self-observation takes practice. It is often hard to check in without judgment. It is easier to begin practicing self-awareness when you're less stressed and anxious. You can apply it to more stressful situations when you are more practiced.

The Observer also practices mindfulness, which is achieved by focusing your awareness on the present moment while calmly acknowledging and accepting your feelings, thoughts, and bodily sensations. Mindfulness decreases stress and increases resilience. We all naturally possess mindfulness, but it becomes more readily available when you practice it regularly, usually through meditation.

The practice of meditation can involve sitting comfortably, focusing on your breathing, and bringing your mind's attention to the present without drifting into thoughts about the past or the future. There are lots of opportunities to practice throughout your day – when walking, driving, or showering, for example. The objective is to be as fully present in the moment as possible. Three words sum it up: be here now. This allows you to disengage from worries, upsets, or concerns, and can help you regain perspective and a more profound sense of self.

The Questioner

The Questioner is curious and will challenge the status quo. They use their imagination, think outside the box, and question existing ways of doing things. The focus on questioning leads to the identification of solutions rather than a focus on the past. If you can develop this aptitude, it will help you be resilient in a world of constant change.

You are at your best when you are a Questioner looking to discover new ways of working. You can become a specialist in something, but the rate of change will make you irrelevant unless you continue to learn.

Organizations that can adapt are more likely to survive in the face of constant change, but they can only do this if everyone asks questions and is curious. Questions like:

- Why are we doing it this way?
- How can we do this better?
- Who can help us?
- Why?
- Why not?

It also means looking to the future and asking:

- What's next?
- Why don't we do this?
- What if?

The Questioner also has the potential to become a great connector, as they discover what other people do and how their work supports that of others.

The Believer

Believers are confident in their abilities and are resilient as a result. Believing in yourself is at the heart of resilience. Self-efficacy is the strong, positive belief that you have the capacity and the skills to achieve your goals.

Psychologist Albert Bandura[13] defined self-efficacy as "one's belief in one's ability to succeed in specific situations or accomplish a task."[14] Bandura's social cognitive theory states that people with high self-efficacy – those who believe they can perform well – tend to see difficult tasks as challenges to be mastered instead of obstacles to avoid.

Bandura identified four sources of efficacy beliefs:

- **Mastery experiences:** The experience of mastering tasks increases your self-efficacy. The secret here is setting small and incremental goals to maintain motivation and enable task mastery over time.

- **Vicarious experiences:** Watching other people like you is an important source of self-efficacy. When others succeed through sustained effort, it leads you to believe that you can do the same.

- **Verbal persuasion:** Other people, such as friends and colleagues, can strengthen your belief that you have what it takes to succeed. This means you are more likely to put in the effort and sustain it when problems arise.

- **Emotional and physiological states:** Your emotional and physiological states will influence how you perceive your self-efficacy. Depression, stress, and anxiety will all influence how you feel about your ability to succeed. Being able to reduce or control negative emotions, such as stress, can boost self-efficacy.

The Realistic Optimist

The Realistic Optimist believes that things can change for the better. Optimism helps increase resilience by reducing negative thought patterns. Note that this is different to the idealistic optimist, who has their head in the clouds and hopes things will turn out okay.

The idealistic optimist believes that success will come to them if they just visualize it hard enough. On the other hand, The Realistic Optimist believes they will succeed but only with hard work, planning, and persistence. They don't visualize an easy path to success; they think seriously about probable obstacles and how to overcome them.

The Realistic Optimist can make a real difference. When pessimists face challenges or obstacles, they give up. When The Realistic Optimist faces challenges or obstacles, they try harder. They propel themselves toward the challenge, find ways to overcome it, and ultimately achieve their goals. When you are an optimist, you think, feel, and behave in a way that creates conditions for success.

Psychologist Gabriele Oettingen performed research on positive thinking and realistic optimism in 1991. She asked twenty-five overweight women enrolled in a weight loss program how likely they were to reach their goal. She found that those confident of success lost twenty-six pounds more than the self-doubters. Interestingly, the women who believed they would achieve their goal within a short period lost twenty-four pounds less than those who recognized that the weight loss journey would take considerable effort.[15]

You can nurture realistic optimism. When faced with a new and potentially daunting task, focus on combining a positive attitude with a candid assessment of the problems and challenges that might await you. Visualize your success and the steps you will take to achieve that success. Realistic optimism protects you from giving up when the going gets tough. If something gets in your way, you have the confidence to knuckle down and look for a solution.

The Adapter

The Adapter is resilient because they are flexible when change and uncertainty are present. In a volatile, uncertain, complex, and ambiguous world of constant change, the ability to continually adapt is vital. Adaptability is key for individuals and organizations alike. Non-adaptive behavior will kill an organization. Success comes from the ability of the people within it to adapt to new ways of thinking and working, and to do so cohesively while remaining calm, attentive, and confident.

Being adaptable reduces anxiety and stress. When you can anticipate and be ready for change, you can modify your attitude and expectations accordingly. Change doesn't need to throw you; it just becomes the

norm. You can adapt your thinking and coping style, and respond to events rather than react to them. Adaptability means you are open to new ideas. You can work independently or as part of a team and reprioritize as needed. You can change direction along the way.

When you are adaptable, you will gain more recognition and trust. People don't see you as someone who panics when faced with change. In fact, you will grow because you will be more likely to take on new challenges.

The Achiever

The Achiever has a sense of purpose, which is essential to resilience. A sense of purpose is your driver and feeds your intrinsic motivation. It gives meaning to your work and increases your engagement in the workplace, which, in turn, boosts your mental well-being.

According to researchers Jane E. Dutton and Amy Wrzesniewski, you can find a sense of purpose in your current job. In an article published in the *Academy of Management Review* in 2001,[16] they coined the term "job crafting," which is about turning your job into one you love. Job crafting involves redefining your job to incorporate your values, beliefs, strengths, and passions.

You can choose to do one or all of the three parts of job crafting:

Rethink the task: You can rethink what you do at work, also known as task crafting, whereby you add, emphasize, or redesign tasks. For example, you may be interested in communication and collaboration, so you add active participation on the organization's collaboration platform as a regular task. If you already have tasks that you enjoy, you can emphasize them by devoting more time and energy to them. Redesigning tasks means you look for ways to re-engineer existing tasks to make them more meaningful.

Rethink the people: You can craft your interactions with others at work in ways that foster meaningfulness by altering with whom and how you form connections and relationships. For example, researchers found that when hospital cleaners increased their interaction with patients and their families, they experienced more appreciation and enacted the role of caregiver, which elevated the sense of meaningfulness they derived from their work.

Rethink the perception: The third part of job crafting is creating meaningfulness regarding how you think about your job. For example, you can find more meaningfulness by focusing on specific tasks and relationships that are significant or valuable to you.

The Celebrant

The Celebrant celebrates both successes and setbacks.

By celebrating successes, you can develop a success mindset. Celebrate successes no matter how small. There may be more to do, but stop and celebrate what you have achieved. Keep telling yourself, "I have succeeded," "I am an achiever," and "I can do this because I have done it before and succeeded." Be proud of what you have done. When you celebrate successes, you increase your motivation and resilience.

If you have large goals, break them down into smaller tasks or actions you can celebrate once you have achieved them. When you anticipate success or achieve success and celebrate, you release dopamine into your brain. It feels good and you want more. Dopamine contributes to feelings of pleasure and satisfaction as part of the reward system. When you celebrate successes openly, it gives others the chance to join in and feel motivated.

As previously said, The Celebrant celebrates successes *and* setbacks. I prefer to use the word "setback" rather than "failure." Thomas Edison (inventor and businessman)[17] said, "I have not failed. I've just found 10,000 ways that won't work." If you have found 10,000 ways that don't work, you have learned from them and have a better understanding of what will work. Every time you have a setback, you are closer to success. It may not feel like it, but you will be closer than you think.

You may feel upset, disappointed, or even frustrated by setbacks. The problem with these feelings is they stop you from having another go, so you feel a real sense of failure. If you celebrate setbacks as a learning opportunity and a step closer to success, you are more motivated to keep going. It is all about perseverance and resilience. Setbacks impart experience, personal growth, and development. Setbacks give you the biggest dose of feedback. So, celebrate them.

The Humorist

Humor is one of the most powerful tools you have when faced with constant change, stress, and anxiety. You can't be a victim when you are laughing.

Research has shown that humor can alleviate depression and increase physical and emotional well-being.[18] It improves mood, relieves stress and anxiety, releases pent-up feelings of anger and frustration, and positively affects behavior. When you are humorous, you are more likely to make eye contact and be more tactile, increasing your connection with others.

The Humorist uses humor as a coping mechanism to guard against stress and increase resilience. Of course, there is a time, place, and situation when you should use humor. Self-deprecation is the safest form of humor and not only creates laughter but makes you more approachable, as you are showing your vulnerability. So, don't be afraid to make fun of your mistakes and weaknesses. Also, when you can laugh at adversity, you have already distanced yourself from it. You have become an observer of the situation. When you have that psychological distance, you can acknowledge your negative emotions and choose positive responses that help you cope.

Humor can broaden your focus, and, as a result, promote exploration, creativity, innovation, and flexibility in thinking. Humor can help you avoid becoming stuck in feelings of negativity and helplessness so you're better able to see the bigger picture and move forward. Humor is good for individuals and can improve an organization's culture. It helps colleagues connect because shared humor can boost morale and motivation. **Laughter is the best medicine!**

The Futurist

The Futurist maintains a long-term perspective and avoids seeing stressful situations as all-encompassing and overwhelming. The Futurist knows that it will pass. They see a situation in a broader context. They avoid blowing everything out of proportion.

You might not be able to change a current situation, but you can look to the future and perceive how things might improve. Dwelling on the current situation increases stress and decreases resilience. There is nothing wrong with the statement "Live in the moment," but, if that moment is bad, you should look to the future to get through it. The Futurist also does not dwell on negative things that have already happened. The Futurist puts them where they belong – in the past – and moves on.

If you can envision a future where you are not stressed and anxious about what you are experiencing in the present, you can get through it. You can lessen the negative emotions and angst you feel. Try to place yourself in the future and look back at your current situation. This can put the situation into perspective, and it may not look so bad. Distancing yourself is a good psychological method for increasing resilience.

When you anticipate a better future and envisage something to look forward to, you're more likely to feel happier and less stressed before the future arrives (no matter how you feel in the present). Being able to look to the future is an essential way to build resilience.

The Thanker

The Thanker is grateful for everything that has got them to where they are today, instead of focusing solely on the next obstacle. This is important, as many people tend to only see what is in front of them and take those things behind them for granted.

Robert Emmons[19] is a professor of psychology at the University of California. He has authored two books about gratitude and says that even in the worst times, gratitude can help you through them. It can energize, heal, and bring hope. It is hard to understand how gratitude could come naturally during a crisis. Still, Emmons points out that you must distinguish between "feeling" grateful and "being" grateful.

You cannot always control your feelings. But being grateful is a choice. When the going gets tough, gratitude can help you see the bigger picture – life in its entirety. It can stop you from becoming overwhelmed by present and temporary circumstances. Gaining this perspective may not come easy, but continually having a go has enormous benefits. You can be grateful if you can think of the worst times and remember that you made it through.

Gratitude gives you the power to change an obstacle into an opportunity and a loss into a potential gain. You can experience genuine gratitude in the face of your challenges, but whether you do so is your choice. Gratitude is a cornerstone of resilience.

The Revealer

The Revealer turns up as their authentic self.

At times, you may try to be someone other than your real self. Perhaps you have a skewed view that you must adopt a persona so that others will like or respect you. Perhaps you engage in self-presentation and modify your behaviors, emotions, and how others see you.

You may do this for many reasons. You may not feel you can express yourself freely. You may feel that you must have all the answers or you will lose credibility. However, the energy you put into pretending to be someone else is exhausting. It diminishes both your energy and your resilience. Trying to be someone you are not cannot be sustained.

You are your authentic self when everything you do aligns with your goals, values, beliefs, and moral compass. As The Revealer, you reveal your true self. It may make you feel vulnerable, and you may feel that others will see it as a weakness. However, vulnerability looks like courage to everyone else.

When you are afraid to speak up in a meeting or you pretend to understand something, you are not being true to yourself. You are not being authentic. You must bring your authentic self to the workplace. You must be your whole self at work. This can be humbling, as it means recognizing that you are not perfect, but it can also be liberating.

When you are authentic, you dare to ask questions, admit when you don't understand something, ask for help, and make genuine connections. It may not come easy. It can be scary. The voices in your head will tell you that you'll get shot down and that no one will listen. "What if they don't like what I say? What if it diminishes my career progression?" You must stop listening to those voices and be true to yourself.

You must take a risk and believe you are better than those voices. You must stop avoiding situations because you fear making mistakes or failing. To be authentic, you must face those fears and feelings, and deliberately step out of your comfort zone. You must accept that you will experience fear but observe it as a natural response, not a reflection of your lack of ability.

The Reframer

The Reframer can look at a situation in more than one way. When you experience an event, you generally form an initial assumption and interpretation of that event. This is called a frame.

The Reframer looks at the event from different perspectives. They take a situation observed from one angle and view it from another to give it more context. This is called a reframe. The Reframer looks to remove negativity from their perspective and increase positivity by looking for opportunities. Often, you cannot control what happens to you, but you can control how you respond to it.

A great example of reframing is the story of Thomas Watson[20], the founder of IBM. Watson knew that one of his employees had made a mistake that cost the organization ten million dollars. Watson asked for the employee to meet him in his office. As the employee entered the office, he said, "I suppose you want my resignation?" Watson looked at him and said in disbelief, "Are you kidding? We have just spent ten million dollars on your education." Watson reframed, recognizing that the mistake had already occurred and the money was lost. He saw it as an opportunity to recover value from this employee.

Reframing forces you to be more focused, creative, and innovative. It forces you to stand back and see things differently. It increases your resilience in the face of constant change.

Imagine standing on the edge of a train platform. As the train comes through the station at close proximity, the velocity pushes you backward like a shock wave. It is disturbing. But when you stand farther back, the train's speed seems slower and less disturbing. So, depending on where you stand – your vantage point – your perceptions of events, and change itself, can differ.

Reframing is not oblivious to the fact that events you encounter are often difficult, dramatic, and disruptive. But rather than succumb to them and view them as rejection, hardship, damaging, and destructive, you can reframe them. To quote a well-known Zen proverb, "Change how you see and see how you change."

The Listener

Effective listening is critical to building and maintaining resilience. Effective listening can avoid misunderstanding, which, in turn, leads to the avoidance of conflict. Misunderstanding and conflict have no place in a resilient workforce.

Effective listening helps you avoid jumping to unfounded conclusions and making assumptions. To be truly resilient, you must fully understand the context in which you find yourself, the problem or challenge, and the options available. If you make assumptions, you will be off-kilter and make ill-informed decisions.

When under pressure and feeling stressed, you may listen with emotional barriers and not hear what others say. Your emotions and unconscious biases can get in the way. They can turn what someone says into something completely different.

In a stressful environment, it can be easy to become distracted by what is happening around you and not hear a conversation in its entirety. Effective communication and listening go together, but, as the saying goes, "We have two ears and one mouth for a reason." That means you should listen twice as much as you speak.

We'll discuss listening in more detail in "Listening."

Resilient, Part 2

Great leaders have a resilient mindset. They can be resilient in themselves, as you discovered in the previous section, and also build a resilient team through specific attributes. That's the focus of this section, which also includes a real-life example of resilience, both on an individual level and in the context of leadership.

Leadership superpowers to build resilience

Here is a summary of the twenty leadership superpowers for you to build and maintain a resilient team. As mentioned earlier, for more information on each superpower and how to acquire it, refer to the book *Unleash the Resiliator Within – Resilience: A Handbook for Leaders.*[21]

The Leader
Delegation and trust

The Connector
Shared sense of purpose

The Removalist
Remove the mental health stigma

The Director
Clear direction

The Communicator
Effective communication

The Reinforcer
Positive reinforcement

The Includer
Trust and inclusivity

The Reflector
Reflection and retrospective

The Identifier
Identify low resilience

The Modeler
Model resilience

The Nurturer
Trust and respect

The Enquirer
Lead with questions

The Autonomizer
Employee autonomy

The Developer
Culture of learning

The Promoter
Promoting self care

The Restructurer
Cognitive restructuring

The Caretaker
Psychological safety

The Cultivator
Environment of innovation

The Accountant
Personal accountability

The Protector
Lead with care and compassion

Figure 11: Leader superpowers

© 2024 Karen Ferris

The Leader

Building and maintaining a resilient workforce requires leaders, not managers. Warren Bennis[22], one of the pioneers of contemporary leadership studies, has said, "The manager does things right; the leader does the right thing." No more command and control! As you will discover in "Empowering," command and control and authoritarian direction have no place in forming resilient individuals. True leaders surrender control.

Leaders who "get out of the way" provide individuals with autonomy, delegate decision-making, and allow team members to experiment and take calculated risks. If it fails, so be it; learn from it and move on. In contrast, a leader who controls everything without tolerance for risk-taking demotivates employees and stifles innovation and experimentation.

Controlling leaders – who are managers, not leaders – create bottlenecks rather than increase throughput. They signal a lack of trust and confidence. The manager relies on control. The leader inspires trust. There is an argument that leaders lead *and* manage. They inspire as leaders and execute as managers. Ultimately, it's the leadership qualities and capabilities that will establish and preserve resilience.

The leader provides clarity of purpose. People are on the same page when leaders communicate what needs to be done and why. Everyone is working toward the same goal.

The Communicator

The Communicator has excellent communication skills. Effective communication builds positive relationships that promote resilience at work.

The Communicator keeps everyone informed about what is happening. People exhibit far greater resilience when they feel engaged and involved with what is happening rather than feeling kept in the dark.

You'll receive a comprehensive guide on communication in "Listening."

The Identifier

The Identifier identifies the signs of low resilience in employees early and takes immediate action. When an individual shows these signs, it is often due to a mental health issue. It could be the result of stress, anxiety, fatigue, or other factors.

The Identifier constantly monitors for signs of low resilience to take action before the situation worsens. The Identifier looks for the following:

- **Behavior:** When a person's temperament is different from their normal behavior, such as increased irritability, agitation, or cynicism.
- **Motivation:** When a person suddenly lacks motivation for their job, when they previously had a sense of purpose and drive.
- **More mistakes or lapses in judgment:** When a person whom you know is competent and good at their job starts making errors or poor choices.
- **Focus:** When a person demonstrates reduced concentration and is having trouble focusing.
- **Problem-solving:** When a person is becoming overwhelmed by simple problems.
- **Sick leave:** When increased sick leave is being taken and there are higher rates of minor illnesses. When low resilience occurs, it's not uncommon to see a corresponding rise in absenteeism and sick days.
- **Tiredness, weariness, or sleepiness:** The signs include dropping heads, constant yawning, and eyelids that seem to be closing.

- **Interoffice conflict:** When there is a lack of collaboration or simmering feuds between employees, or decreased interaction in meetings and continued unresolved conflict.
- **Planning:** When there is a lack of planning for the future. When demonstrated behavior in responding to daily issues is more reactive than proactive, and there is no anticipation of issues and opportunities.
- **Productivity:** When there is a decrease in productivity for no apparent reason.
- **Morale:** When there is decreased morale, employees start to disengage.
- **Language:** When there is use of defeatist language such as "I can't" or "It won't work."

There is guidance on checking in with employees regarding their well-being in "Empathetic."

The Autonomizer

The Autonomizer provides employees with autonomy – the freedom to do their job their way.

Autonomy gives employees the power to shape their work environment in ways that allow them to perform at their best. The benefit to both the employee and the organization is that employees are happier, more engaged, more committed and motivated, more productive, and less likely to leave the organization. .

We'll discuss this more in "Empowering."

The Caretaker

The Caretaker makes sure there is psychological safety in the workplace.

Psychological safety allows employees to speak up, question decisions, ask for more information, a n d ask for support without fear of being embarrassed or punished by others. When this happens, employees can be resilient in the face of constant change.

We'll discuss psychological safety in more detail in "Empowering."

The Connector

A resilient team is one in which employees have a shared sense of purpose and connectedness. The Connector facilitates this, encouraging cross-functional collaboration to draw on individuals' diverse skills and capabilities. They provide autonomy for teams to solve problems, seize opportunities, experiment, innovate, and make decisions within provided parameters.

Employees will face setbacks, challenges, and high demands during constant change. It means that, as a leader, you must invest in building networks and connecting teams with other teams. You must provide team cohesion through social activities, group training, celebration of individual and team achievements, informal team get-togethers, and a culture of mutual trust and respect.

You encourage employees to reach out to each other for support. You create environments where team members can share openly and fairly, and demonstrate empathy for others. You can leverage the pool of knowledge, skills, expertise, and experience across team disciplines, industries, and geographical boundaries. By creating coalitions of networks, you can connect diverse thinking, ideas, and solutions that lead to positive change and innovation. You can increase the speed at which problems and opportunities get addressed.

The Reinforcer

The Reinforcer reinforces desired behaviors. Positive reinforcement builds resilience.

Many authors have written extensively about reinforcement theory. The basic tenet of reinforcement theory is that behavior is shaped and maintained by its consequences. Employees who are positively reinforced work together more efficiently and harmoniously, and are more resilient in the process.

Effective leaders give positive reinforcement while the employee is doing the job. When you reinforce a behavior at the time performed, it is clear what behavior you are reinforcing. The person receiving the reinforcement also understands which behavior elicited the positive feedback.

The longer the time between the behavior and the reinforcement, the less effective it is. This is exactly why annual performance reviews have little or no impact on behavior. Individual and team resilience can also be supported when employees give positive reinforcement to each other. As a leader, you should

encourage positive feedback at every opportunity.

More on this in "Empowering."

The Modeler

The Modeler models resilience. As a leader, your employees are looking to you to model resilience. They want to see how you deal with constant and uncertain change pressure. They want to see you deal with setbacks, let-downs, and failed attempts at success – and still bounce forward. They will take their cues from you, so they must see you modeling resilient behavior.

Resilient leaders model the following behaviors:

- They are **champions of change.** They don't resist it. They accept that constant change is the norm, and they embrace it. They demonstrate that they are willing to change and lead others to do the same. They see the challenges of constant change as great opportunities.

- They are **quick to change direction.** Resilient leaders quickly make decisions and realize there is no time for procrastination. They decide, and, if it is wrong, they quickly change direction.

- They see **failure as a learning opportunity.** Resilient leaders don't see failure as a setback but as an opportunity to learn and move forward. Rather than dwell on the negative, they look at the positive and examine the lessons learned from the setback.

- They **signal intentions.** They let everyone know what is going on. This requires effective communication that is clear and unambiguous, which allows others to understand changes and new directions (and observe effective communication in the process).

- They **take risks.** They demonstrate that they are prepared to take risks and try new things.

The Developer

The Developer creates a culture of learning. When change is constant and ever-increasing in speed, leaders need to move from training programs to a continuous learning and development model that repeatedly builds employees' skills and provides a range of formal training options.

Leaders must determine the skills available today and the skills needed in the future, and perform a gap analysis. They must then work to address the gap, developing the skills from within the organization before looking externally. Often, organizations are unaware of the talent they possess internally. They should audit skills and develop an internal gig economy. As new requirements emerge, the organization can quickly locate existing employees who have indicated interest in new opportunities and have the skills to meet them. Employees can gain experience and develop new capabilities in ways their current jobs don't allow.

The role of the leader is to help employees continuously learn. It means providing them with the tools and technology they need for increased collaboration, learning on-demand, and the ability to find what they need when they need it from a variety of sources. Leaders must build a growth mindset in employees (there's more information on growth mindsets in "Adaptive"). To quote the late businessman Arie de Geus, "The ability to learn faster than your competitors may be the only sustainable competitive advantage."[23]

The Cultivator

The Cultivator creates an environment for innovation. Employees who do not feel safe contributing through creativity, experimentation, and innovation will have low resilience. Organizations that struggle to stay ahead of the game, due to a lack of innovation, will cease to exist. Therefore, as a leader, you must cultivate an environment where innovation thrives.

Psychological safety is key to innovation. An environment where everyone feels safe to try new things, however crazy they may seem, is imperative. Everyone should feel free and safe to challenge the status quo and suggest potentially better ways of doing business. You must hear every idea and give it space for consideration. It is easy to tear down ideas, but the best people bring bricks to help build something.

We'll discuss psychological safety in more detail in "Empowering."

The Removalist

The Removalist works to remove the stigma of mental health issues in the workplace. Stigma can be one of the greatest barriers to psychological health and safety at work, directly impacting employee resilience.

Employees frequently hold back from seeking help for mental health issues – such as anxiety, stress, or depression – due to concerns that others will see them in a negative light. They fear others will see them as lazy, irresponsible, weak, or dangerous.

As a leader, you must strive to eliminate the stigma so that employees experiencing mental health issues can reach out sooner, access resources, and restore their well-being. Removing the stigma helps employees suffering from mental health conditions, and it encourages other employees to talk about the subject. Here are some points to keep in mind:

- **Be educated and informed:** As a leader, you need to understand what mental health is and what it is not. Seek out training and resources to inform you. Find out if an employee assistance program (EAP) exists in your organization, and, if so, what it can do to help.

- **Use the right language:** Certain words and language can reinforce the stigma around mental health issues. Avoid language such as "She *suffers* from severe anxiety" or "He is *struggling* with depression." The language used should not be emotional. Say it simply: "Mary has anxiety" or "John has depression."

- **Speak up:** If you hear someone talking negatively about a person's mental health, speak up and challenge them. Do not allow others to ostracize those with mental health issues.

- **Foster a supportive team culture:** Foster a team culture that encourages open and honest communication, and can discuss concerns such as stress, anxiety, depression, fatigue, and so on without fear of any negative repercussions or of being judged.

- **Share it:** Other people openly sharing their stories and experiences around mental health can be extremely powerful. Invite speakers to talk to your team or the organization about how they overcame their mental health challenges. If there are people within the organization who have had mental health issues that they have overcome, ask if they would share their stories with others.

The Includer

The Includer builds a resilient team by fostering and modeling trust and inclusivity. The Includer embraces the idea that an inclusive workplace is one in which injury, mental illness, or disability do not present obstacles to a fulfilling work life. The Includer builds inclusivity through the creation of diverse teams.

Diversity is not just diversity of age, cultural background, physical ability, race, religion, sex, and sexual orientation – it also means diversity of thinking. Diversity of people and thinking results in a broader knowledge base, a variety of perspectives, different cognitive mindsets, and creativity. This can reduce errors and enhance problem-solving. When all team members think alike, they may overlook errors and leave problems unresolved. This is the result of groupthink.

Imagine that, within your team, you have a young university graduate working alongside someone who has been with the organization for over thirty years. It would mean your team has a broad knowledge base, which will enhance resilience. Teams that include a range of voices and perspectives are better placed to innovate, take risks, solve problems creatively, bounce back from failures, and turn challenges into opportunities.

The Nurturer

The Nurturer builds a culture of trust and respect. When there is trust and respect, employees are connected. They feel safe to express their feelings, knowing their voice will be heard and valued. This results in resilience.

Leaders must listen to their employees and seek their feedback regularly. Everyone should feel comfortable sharing with you and their peers. Provide education on effective communication, listening techniques, and how to lead with empathy.

As a leader, you have to demonstrate that you care. You have to be accountable for any commitments you have made. When employees give you feedback, you must show that you have heard them. If you cannot act on their feedback, tell them why.

The Nurturer actively encourages team members to support each other. Every team member should be able to present as their authentic self.

The Promoter

The Promoter promotes self-care. You may forget to look after yourself in your busy, always-on life. However, when you don't look after yourself, this can lead you to become stressed, anxious, fatigued, and burnt out.

Self-care is core to your resilience as a leader in a world of constant change. You need to look after yourself and encourage others to do the same. This means leading by example.

Encourage employees to engage in activities that help them focus on their senses. These need to be activities they prefer – not everyone likes yoga! There is no one-size-fits-all; there are many sizes to choose from. These include (but are not limited to):

- **Mindfulness** to improve focus and concentration.
- **Meditation** to increase awareness and gain a healthy sense of perspective.
- **Massage** for relaxation and stress relief.
- **Regular exercise** to boost memory and thinking, as well as physical well-being.
- **Technology detoxes** to improve sleep.
- **Alone time** to spark creativity, build mental strength, and increase empathy and productivity.
- **Regular breaks** to refresh and recharge.

As a leader, you can also offer employees time management, stress management, and resilience training.

The Accountant

Good leadership requires real accountability. The Accountant takes personal accountability for their choices, behaviors, and actions. The Accountant does not point fingers at others when things don't go as planned. They take ownership and act accordingly.

Accountable leaders do the following four things:

1. They are honest. Accountable leaders are prepared to admit their mistakes and say, "I stuffed up." They are honest about their strengths and weaknesses, and work on personal improvement.

2. They seek input. Accountable leaders know they don't need to have all the answers, so they seek input from team members, peers, and colleagues. They ask for help in overcoming a problem or seizing an opportunity.

3. They apologize. Accountable leaders readily say "I'm sorry" when something they were accountable for has gone wrong. They are prepared to make things right and commit to the actions needed.

4. They are decisive. Accountable leaders do not procrastinate for fear of making a wrong decision. They are resolute in their decision-making.

Leaders can build accountability in their teams by doing the following:

1. Build trust. You have to trust your team to do the right thing. If you micromanage, you're effectively saying, "I don't trust you."

2. Provide clarity. Make sure everyone is clear about your expectations.

3. **Communicate**. Keep the team focused and accountable through regular communication and feedback.

4. **Collaborate**. Team members need to work together, and they should hold each other accountable. A regular team catch-up is essential to ensure that everyone has completed their tasks as promised or to identify any obstacles that need addressing.

5. **Provide visibility**. Make all progress visible. If things are not going to plan, don't immediately lay blame. Instead, be curious. What happened? What could we have done differently? Give equal focus to the things that have gone well and those that haven't.

The Director

The Director provides clear direction for themselves and their employees, but not at the expense of employee autonomy. They provide direction without being prescriptive or micromanaging. When setbacks occur, they can get everyone back on track and working toward shared goals. Everyone needs to know where they are going. If they don't, there is uncertainty and confusion, which lowers resilience.

As a leader, you set direction and create a shared sense of purpose where everyone is heading in the same direction. The direction must be crystal clear. You must describe it in simple language, outlining how everyone will move forward.

A leader's direction for a team or organization is often called the North Star. In the past, mariners made their way through seas and oceans using celestial bodies such as the sun, moon, and stars. Polaris, also known as the North Star, was the most popular and reliable. A North Star is the positive vision that a leader creates and shares. It points everyone in the right direction.

The direction must include the following:

- **Vision:** Your "North Star statement", providing clarity on the direction you're taking.
- **Context:** Any relevant background information regarding the direction.
- **Expectations:** The expectations of everyone involved, including the outcomes and timeframes.
- **The why:** The reason you are heading in that direction. The "why" is often overlooked in preference of explaining the "what" and the "how."

The Reflector

The Reflector provides time for individual and team reflection. After experiencing a challenge, change, or event perceived as stressful, the Reflector takes time to reflect on:

- What went well?
- What didn't go so well?
- What did we learn?
- What could we do better?
- What were the negative experiences?
- What were the positive experiences?
- How can we increase our resilience?

Use this as a post-event briefing to improve resilience. The Reflector encourages every team member to reflect on their recent experiences. Discussion about the challenge, and how employees coped, is encouraged. This activity helps team members to support each other. The process can include action planning for the team. You can conduct this activity after a significant event or a series of low-impact events that may have left the team feeling depleted and fatigued by change. These reflection sessions are often called retrospectives.

The Enquirer

The Enquirer asks questions – a lot of questions. When leaders have conversations based on asking questions rather than giving directions, employees feel valued, motivated, and empowered. It helps build resilience in the team. When you ask employees questions, you tell them you are interested in what they say.

There are two types of questions. One looks at what has already happened, and the other looks to the

future. Looking at what has happened garners employee perspectives about the event(s). The "already happened" questions might include:

- How did that make you feel?
- What challenges did you face?
- What would success have looked like?

The forward-looking questions might include:

- What could we do better?
- What should we stop doing?
- What should we do next?
- What ideas do you have?

When you ask questions, you create a conversation with many different voices. Those voices are curious, creative, innovative, and engaged.

The Restructurer

The Restructurer uses cognitive restructuring to challenge negative and reactive thinking. What you say and how you say it can shape how you – and others – think. What you think can increase the intensity of your emotions and how you perceive difficult situations. Therefore, the use of negative language can create negative emotions, which will result in low resilience.

Leaders and the individuals in their teams can use cognitive restructuring to change the way they think about situations. Leaders should challenge negative language such as:

- "I can't do it."
- "It isn't even worth trying."
- "I am stressed with the uncertainty of it all."
- "I will just avoid challenges as it is easier than facing them."

These are all negative predictions. As a leader, you should pay attention when they happen. When employees think this way, it is hard for them to see any positive outcomes.

As a leader, you can do the following:

- Calm the situation. Guide your employee to a quiet place and get them to breathe deeply.
- Ask your employee about their feelings and what has triggered them. Be mindful that negative language like "I can't do that" can stem from low self-esteem and lack of confidence. Therefore, it is important to determine what is underpinning the negative language. When you know the triggers, you can manage them.

- If your employee makes unfounded assumptions about a current or future situation, you need to help them reframe and look at the situation more positively. You can do this by offering a different perspective for the employee to consider.

The Protector

The Protector protects the team by ensuring it has the capabilities and resources to be resilient. The Protector's language and behaviors say, "I care about you, and I value your contribution."

Leaders who protect their employees support and stand up for them. They make sure their employees have everything they need to get the job done. Employees are not left to fend for themselves and flounder. When leaders protect employees, they develop and coach them to be their best.

Leaders must protect their employees, wherever possible, from anything that might lower their resilience. This includes unnecessary distractions, poor work prioritization, work overload, unclear goals and outcomes, and unconsidered demands from other parts of the organization. Leaders offer protection by encouraging employee personal well-being and modeling resilient behaviors. They provide autonomy and self-direction, and are consistent, fair, honest, and transparent. They provide opportunities for employees to recharge.

Real-world example: Abraham Lincoln

Abraham Lincoln was elected as the sixteenth president of the United States in 1861 and served until his assassination in 1865. He was forty-nine years old when elected, and his resilience is what got him there. The events leading up to his election are known as the Lincoln "Failures" list. Many versions of the list exist, including this one from Abraham Lincoln Online.[24]

1832	Lost job
	Defeated for state legislature
1833	Failed in business
1835	Sweetheart died
1836	Had nervous breakdown
1838	Defeated for speaker
1843	Defeated for nomination to Congress
1848	Lost renomination
1849	Rejected for land officer
1854	Defeated for US Senate
1856	Defeated for nomination for Vice President
1858	Defeated again for US Senate

During these years, Lincoln did have some successes, such as being elected to Congress in 1846 and admitted to practice law in the US Supreme Court in 1849. However, the election defeat after election defeat could have quashed his determination to be elected to public office. But it did not deter him, and his resilience saw him through his decades-long quest.

During his time as president, Lincoln continued to be resilient. He was president during the Civil War. It divided America, and tens of thousands lost their lives. He governed at a time when Americans fought Americans. Lincoln was able to reflect on his setbacks and learn from them. Drawing on his past experiences, inner strength, and acquired wisdom, he maintained perspective and composure during a time that would have broken others. He was resilient.

Empathetic

Disruption is a constant in the workplace, whether it's caused by economic headwinds, corporate downsizing, pandemic recovery, accelerating digital transformation, geopolitical tensions – the list goes on and on. Disruption can make people feel uncomfortable, scared, concerned, anxious, and stressed. Organizational success will depend on leaders with an empathetic mindset.

Empathy is the ability to understand and perhaps share the feelings of another person. Compassionate action must accompany empathy. Empathy without action is empty. Empathy is critical to building positive relationships with others. When you possess empathy, you can understand other people's perspectives, needs, and intentions. Empathy means you care about other people.

In the workplace, empathy is crucial because it creates an environment where employees feel heard, valued, understood, and cared for. It builds trust, increases effective collaboration, and improves communication.

Research by Catalyst[25] found the following benefits of empathy in the workplace:

- Empathy drives productivity, life-work integration, and positive work experiences.
- Empathy boosts productivity.
- Empathy reduces burnout.

- Employees with empathetic managers and leaders are more innovative and engaged than those with less empathetic managers and leaders.
- Empathetic leaders respect employees' life circumstances.
- Empathetic leaders support both the personal and professional needs of employees.
- Empathetic leaders foster inclusion.
- Senior leader empathy reduces employee intent to leave.

So, how do you become an empathetic leader?

Cultivating empathy in leadership

Empathy requires a high level of emotional intelligence. For example, in a difficult or challenging conversation with an employee, you must be able to put aside your and the other person's feelings to view the situation subjectively. The emotions in the conversation do not control the outcome.

That's not to say you shouldn't show concern. On the contrary, empathetic leaders demonstrate a genuine concern for others, whether it's a person's mental state, a challenge they face, or a professional or personal situation. They reach out, ask questions, and, when they understand, they help. They provide support, guidance, coaching, motivation, comfort, or whatever may be required to help remedy the situation in which the other person finds themselves. Only by being empathetic can you truly understand the other person's situation and offer the appropriate assistance.

Here are some ways to cultivate empathy as a leader.

Learn

The first step for you as a leader and your team is understanding what empathy is and is not. You gain understanding through learning and development. The key to any empathy learning and development program is that it incorporates experiential learning and learning transfer. Experiential learning means that the learner learns through experience and reflection while undertaking the learning. Learning transfer means employees can immediately apply the knowledge in the workplace. The program should not be "set and forget." The program should provide opportunities for learners to share their experiences (good and bad) and hone their empathy skills.

When I develop empathy with a leader and their team, I like to do it as a group. This allows the team to work together on developing their skills as a unit. They can experience, share, reflect, support, question, and grow alongside each other. They can undertake activities and role-play to practice and hone their empathy skills. This facilitates ongoing discussion and exploration in the workplace. Team members can call out positive examples of empathetic behavior and examples where there is room for improvement.

I also recommend reading books such as *Dare to Lead* by Brené Brown and *Man's Search for Meaning* by Viktor Frankl, and using resources such as *Harvard Business Review*, which curated ten original articles about empathy and turned them into a book: *Emotional Intelligence: Empathy*.

Listen

You cannot be empathetic if you do not actively listen to what the other person is saying. To actively listen, you must be fully present in the moment, focus on what you are hearing, avoid all distractions, refrain from interruption, and seek clarification on what you have heard. You should remain impartial and non-judgmental.

I'd like to share an example of a great leader with exceptional listening skills, but you're unlikely to have heard her name before. Máiréad M. Barrett left Clonmel, Ireland, for New York in 1967, at the age of seventeen, to join the Ursuline Order of Tildonk. The order was committed to providing a safe haven for families of refugees and many others living in poverty. By listening to their stories with empathy, she realized that these shelters were only providing a short-term fix to a problem that needed a real, lasting solution. In her words, "We were attempting to put a Band-Aid on a hemorrhage."[26]

She had a vision. She realized that to achieve progressive and successful outcomes for 100 per cent of the people with whom they engaged, they needed to combine the disciplines of education and social work. The utilization of trained educators and social workers allowed them to engage their clients while keeping them motivated and inspired to secure work that would ultimately help them support themselves and their families.

Her vision was realized when she formed New Ground, and it opened its doors on January 15, 1991. Today, New Ground's structure includes professional social workers and educators as the primary staff who interact with the families and veterans they serve.

The figures speak for themselves. Since 1991:

- 100 per cent of families have increased their household income while participating in the Long Term Housing and JumpStart Programs.
- Eighty-four per cent of all families have achieved most or all of their goals toward self-sufficiency and have secured permanent stable housing.[27]

Máiréad has received numerous awards and honors for her work. For outstanding work in education, she received the Martin Luther King Jr. Award. She also received the Women of Distinction Award for her unparalleled contribution to society on Long Island. She is my sister-in-law.

Check in

You must continually check in with your team by asking, "Are you okay?" or "Is everything okay?" If the answer is "No," follow up with an open question like "What is troubling you?" or "What is on your mind?" If the answer is "Yes," still follow up with an open question to confirm that the other person is not just saying "Yes" because they think that is what you want to hear. Ask them how their project is going, how they feel the team is working together, or what improvements they think could be made to the working environment.

When you establish a connection with your team, you will find that you can anticipate their needs and recognize when they may need extra help or support. Watch out for changes in demeanor, language, or emotional state that may indicate something is wrong.

I had this experience a few years ago. I received an email from a colleague in response to one from me. I had asked for some guidance on where to find out more information about a particular project. The answer I received was short and to the point. I thought it was abrupt. This behavior was out of character, and I sensed something might be wrong.

As we were working remotely, I called my colleague and said, "Sarah, are you okay?" The response I got was a "Uh-huh." I asked again, but this time I said, "Sarah, are you *really* okay?" There was a pause, and then Sarah began to cry. I didn't say anything and just let Sarah take her time. Eventually, she told me that her ten-year-old daughter had tried to take her own life the previous evening. The daughter was physically okay but had some mental problems. Sarah and her partner had done everything right, and their daughter would get the necessary help and counseling. In the meantime, Sarah needed a virtual shoulder to cry on, which was my job. I supported her by being there, and I checked in regularly to see how she was coping. She knew she had someone in her corner who cared.

Other tell-tale signs could be if a team member takes more sick leave than usual. Look out for team members exhibiting distraction in meetings, a lack of focus, low energy levels, and a fall in productivity. Watch for those tell-tale signs and reach out. All you may have to do is listen and provide support. I know some people who are afraid to ask, "Are you okay?" in case the answer they get back is "No." They fear they will not know what to do. Remember, no one expects you to be a medical professional, psychologist, or psychiatrist. You are there to offer support, which could be finding the right person to help.

Create a safe space

You must create an environment where people feel safe expressing their feelings. Your employees must trust you if they are going to confide in you. They must feel secure that you will not judge, reprimand, or think less of them. There are two factors at play here. One is that you must create an environment of psychological safety. The other is that there must be no stigma attached to mental health in your workplace. As discussed earlier, many employees who experience mental health issues are reluctant to reach out for help for fear that others will view them negatively. They fear being seen as weak and not up to the job. Your job is to remove the stigma. See "Resilient, Part 2 – The Removalist."

I was asked to help a leader in a large manufacturing company who had just inherited, in their words, "a dysfunctional team." The team made many mistakes, tried to hide them, and was reluctant to discuss the situation. There was clearly a lack of psychological safety. I had numerous conversations with team members, and those who were prepared to speak up confirmed the situation. The previous manager would berate a team member in front of the rest of the team when a mistake was made. If a new team member asked the manager for help, they would receive a belittling response along the lines of "read the manual." When a team member showed initiative and suggested a process improvement, they would be immediately shut down and told that they did not have the tenure to suggest changes.

The new leader would have a real challenge turning the situation around, but she was determined to do it. With my support, we developed an approach.

She started by discussing what she believed to be her strengths and the areas in which she needed to improve. She was prepared to be vulnerable and acknowledge her own fallibility. She would say to the team, "I am not sure of the best way to do this. What do you think?" or "Can you help me with this?" This made the team members feel more comfortable asking for help. In team meetings, she invited the team to challenge her decisions, explaining that she did not always have all the answers and there were members of the team far more knowledgeable in specific areas.

Initiative and innovation were encouraged, and the team was constantly told to question the status quo and that every idea would be heard. She asked a lot of questions – and I mean *a lot* – which not only told the team she was genuinely interested in what they had to say but also encouraged them to speak up.

She used positive reinforcement to recognize and encourage more of the behaviors she wanted to see. She ensured she was available to support them when they needed help or guidance. She always had an open mind and was non-judgmental. See "Resilient, Part 2 – The Reinforcer."

The most powerful way she created an environment of psychological safety was to make it okay to make mistakes. She framed mistakes as learning opportunities, saying, "If we are not making mistakes, we are not making progress." She openly admitted her mistakes and shared what she had learned. When mistakes were made, she asked the team, "What can we learn from this, and how can we make sure it is better next time?"

Gradually, the team members openly shared the mistakes they made, and the team collectively worked on solutions. The team changed from dysfunctional to high-performing over a period of ten months.

Consider using CBT

A technique you can use to help an employee voice how they are feeling is cognitive behavior therapy (CBT).[28] You do not have to be a medical practitioner to use it. Once you have acknowledged your employee's poor mental health, you will have raised their awareness of their mood, and you have also validated how they are feeling.

This tool can prompt open conversations and help your employees understand how negative thoughts cause specific feelings, behaviors, and physical reactions. There are connections between what you think, feel, and do, and how your body reacts. Changing one can affect the others. There is no specific order in which this happens, but your thoughts tend to come first.

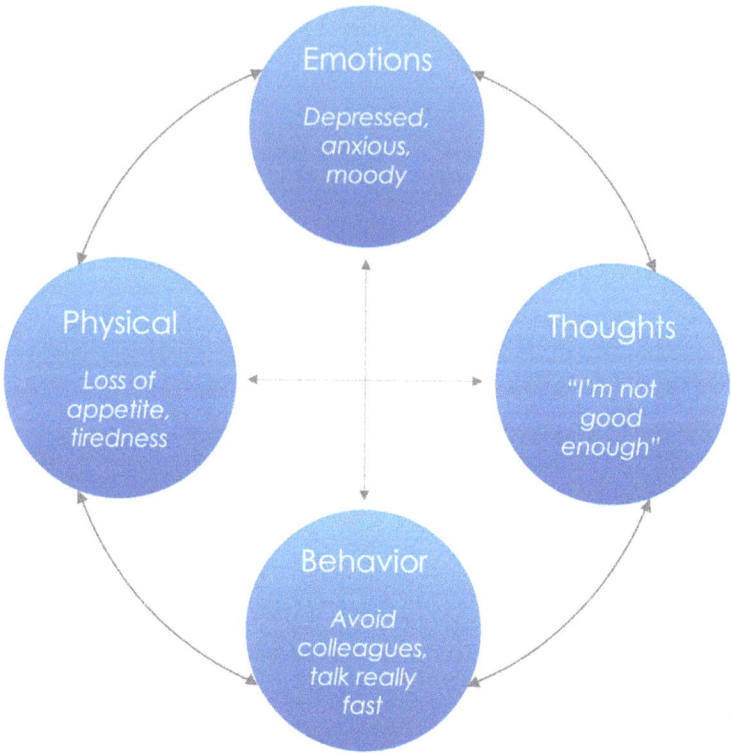

Figure 12: CBT tool

Using this tool, you can ask your employee to identify the thinking patterns or behaviors causing them mental distress.

1. What emotions are they feeling? These could include anger, sadness, anxiety, and stress.

2. What are the thoughts in their head? They could include "They are going to laugh at me," "I am going to fail," and "Something bad is about to happen."

3. What is happening physically? Physical responses could include tense shoulders, sweating, fast breathing, a racing heart, dizziness, loss of appetite, or lethargy.

4. What behaviors are they exhibiting? They could include avoidance, disengaging socially, taking sick leave, or procrastinating.

The patterns can be self-perpetuating. For example, an employee could fear presenting in front of the team. The emotion is fear. The thought is, "I cannot do this. They will laugh at me." The physical reaction is shaking and a racing heart. The behavior is avoidance. When you next ask your employee to give a presentation, the cycle will repeat itself, and the danger is the fear intensifies. You must help your employee to break the cycle. When you engage in a conversation about an employee's mental well-being, you must provide a safe environment where your employees can voice their feelings without fear of being judged.

The CBT tool can help you as a leader understand your challenging situations and your problematic reactions to them. You can help your employee by sharing the thoughts that influenced your emotions, behaviors, and physical response, making it okay for your employee to do the same.

You can look at each aspect of the tool and work out how to break the cycle. Let's say that you have noticed a change in the behavior of Aditi, one of your team members. Her personality is usually bubbly, and she is a great team player. Recently, she has become withdrawn and is not engaging with her teammates like usual.

Firstly, you acknowledge the change in behavior and your concern for Aditi's mental health. You have now raised her awareness of her behavior and stated that it is okay and that you want to help. You validate how Aditi is feeling. Then, you can explore how she is feeling by using the tool. What is she thinking? How is she feeling? How is this affecting her behavior, and how is she reacting physically?

It becomes apparent that Aditi's youngest child is having problems at school and has started to exhibit disruptive behavior. The school has recommended twelve weeks of counseling and therapy to remedy the situation. Aditi believes the school will expel her child if they do not get help. She is worried, distracted, and anxious. A key worry is that as a single mother, she is the only one who can (or should) go with her child to the counseling sessions. Attendance at these sessions will mean time out from work, and she also needs time to give her child the emotional support they need right now. She fears she will lose her job.

You empathize. You have helped Aditi surface her worries and fears. As her leader, you are in a position to allay the fears of losing her job. You can reassure her that it will not happen, and you will rearrange her work duties around her child's immediate needs. You will review the arrangement regularly to determine if any adjustment is needed. You may not be able to help Aditi identify the right counseling service or advise her on providing the support her child needs, but you can support her as she navigates those things. You ensure that Aditi knows you can provide support whenever she needs it, and you will check in regularly to see how she is managing.

Call it out

Everyone must be encouraged to call it out when they see someone not being empathetic. The call-out involves intentionally creating an environment of empathetic behavior and establishing a charter where everyone agrees to constructively and respectfully call out non-empathetic behavior.

Often, the person who has shown a lack of empathy may have been under pressure from deadlines or suffering mental health issues, and they have reverted to old patterns of behavior. Often, the response is a thanks for calling it out and noting that they could have done better.

I encountered an issue like this with a government client. Someone asked Carlos to do a presentation for around 300 people. Carlos was stressed as he suffered severe anxiety when he had to speak in front of a large crowd. He confided in me that his manager, Dimitri, was getting fed up with the situation. This behavior was a little surprising as Dimitri was generally a good leader who listened to, and cared for, his team.

I found time to talk to Dimitri and mentioned my conversation with Carlos. Dimitri told me he had been asked to take on higher-level duties and was under a lot of pressure in his acting position. He needed Carlos to step up and take on more responsibility, including tasks Dimitri would have been doing himself a few weeks ago. He acknowledged his impatience and lack of empathy. We discussed what it would look like if he took compassionate action. The actions included Dimitri explaining his lack of empathy, not putting Carlos under unnecessary stress by delegating tasks he could not do, and discussing options with Carlos to increase his confidence with public speaking, such as enrolling in Toastmasters.

Be intentional

You must work to make empathy an integral part of the company culture. It does not just happen by osmosis. It must be intentional. You must create an organization-wide intent to learn how to be genuinely empathetic. Everyone, including CEOs, must be able to demonstrate empathy.

A Businesssolver survey found that sixty-nine per cent of CEOs believe it's their job to build empathy in the workplace, yet seventy-nine per cent say they struggle to be empathetic. What's more, seventy-seven per cent of CEOs worry they will lose respect if they're too empathetic, a nine-point increase compared to 2021.[29]

That last statistic is frightening. It indicates that many executives still consider the human side of leadership, such as vulnerability, humility, caring, and empathy, as signs of weakness when, in fact, they are signs of courage.

The same survey found that two out of three employees believe employers view people with mental health issues as "weak" or "a burden." Almost sixty per cent of employees fear reaching out to a manager or HR person about a mental health issue could negatively affect their job security.[30]

If there is a stigma around mental health, there must be an intentional effort and commitment to eradicate it. The World Health Organization defines stigma as:

"A distinguishing mark establishing a demarcation between the stigmatized person and others attributing negative characteristics to this person. The stigma attached to mental illness often leads to social exclusion and discrimination and creates an additional burden for the affected individual."[31]

With this in mind, leaders must:

- Learn more about mental health and how best to respond in the workplace.
- Minimize the risk of mental health issues such as job stress due to an excessive workload, long hours, unclear roles and responsibilities, or unsafe working conditions.

- Educate teams about mental health through online resources, training, presentations, and so on.
- Have open and honest discussions about mental health at work. Share experiences that encourage others to do the same.
- Have regular conversations with staff and check in on their well-being.

Enable others to show empathy

You must encourage everyone in your team (and organization more broadly) to treat each other as human beings. We are people with good days and bad days, people with worries and concerns, people who have responsibilities for others, people who laugh and cry, people who strive to be better, people from different backgrounds with different cultural contexts, and people with different life experiences.

Everyone must recognize that emotional transformation is an ongoing journey. Everyone must work on themselves to deepen self-awareness to manage their emotions and help others navigate theirs. Enable everyone to learn and demonstrate empathy. Do this through ongoing conversation, education, and development.

A small team I worked with had recently formulated their team charter, which consisted of a set of guiding principles. They were proud of their accomplishment and were starting to hold each other accountable for upholding the principles. I demonstrated the need for empathy in order to live by each of the principles, and this made them keen to better understand and share the feelings of one another.

For example, they had a principle of listening and keeping an open mind. This could not be achieved without empathy. They had to recognize that team members may see things from different perspectives, and, therefore, they had to listen without judgment. They had to empathize to understand the feelings of their teammates. Another principle was creating a safe space for everyone. This required empathy to understand what their teammates were experiencing and support them when needed. They needed empathy to appreciate that not everyone is the same; different people may have different communication and working styles.

Real-world example: Mark Cuban

Amid soaring inflation in 2022, businessman and former principal owner of the Dallas Mavericks, Mark Cuban, created an online pharmacy to tackle high medication prices. When asked why he created the pharmacy, Cuban spoke with a deep empathy for consumers, stating, "It's just wrong that people have to choose between eating, you know, their rent, and taking their medications."

Cuban was able to put himself in the position of a struggling person, even though he is a billionaire, and, as a result of this empathy, he created an online business that can help.[32]

Mindful

The mindful mindset enables a leader to be present, in the moment, calm, self-aware, compassionate, and accepting without judgment.

This definition is from mindful.org: "Mindfulness is the basic human ability to be fully present, aware of where we are and what we're doing, and not overly reactive or overwhelmed by what's going on around us."[33] Mindfulness can reduce anxiety and stress, increase focus and attention, improve relationships, and elevate creativity. It does this by helping you to be self-aware, to self-regulate, and to practice emotional control.

Building self-awareness

Self-awareness is how you experience and understand your character, feelings, motives, and desires. Shelley Duval and Robert A. Wicklund developed the theory of self-awareness in their 1972 publication *A Theory of Objective Self Awareness*.[34] The theory states that when you focus on yourself, you evaluate and compare your current behavior to your internal standards and values. You then have objective self-awareness. You can objectively assess yourself, and, in doing so, judge the correctness of your thoughts and behaviors. When you are truly mindful, you do this daily.

Tasha Eurich is an organizational psychologist, researcher, and *New York Times* bestselling author. Research by Eurich and her colleagues found that while most people *believe* they are self-aware, very few actually are. They estimate that only around ten to fifteen per cent meet the criteria of being self-aware. The findings could help leaders to see themselves more clearly.[35]

Eurich and her team have determined that there are two types of self-awareness: internal self-awareness and external self-awareness.

According to the team, internal self-awareness "... represents how clearly we see our own values, passions, aspirations, fit with our environment, reactions (including thoughts, feelings, behaviors, strengths, and weaknesses), and impact on others." Internal self-awareness brings higher job and relationship satisfaction, personal and social control, and happiness. It is also negatively related to anxiety, stress, and depression.

External self-awareness is knowing how others view you regarding your thoughts, feelings, behaviors, strengths, and weaknesses. People with external self-awareness are more skilled at empathy and understanding other people's perspectives. This is particularly advantageous for leaders. The researchers state, "For leaders who see themselves as their employees do, their employees tend to have a better relationship with them, feel more satisfied with them, and see them as more effective in general."

The research found no relationship between internal and external self-awareness. However, it did identify four leadership archetypes and each one has opportunities for improvement. Eurich provides an "Insight Quiz" to determine where you stand in each category: https://www.insight-book.com/quiz

The Four Self-Awareness Archetypes

This 2x2 maps internal self-awareness (how well you know yourself) against external self-awareness (how well you understand how others see you).

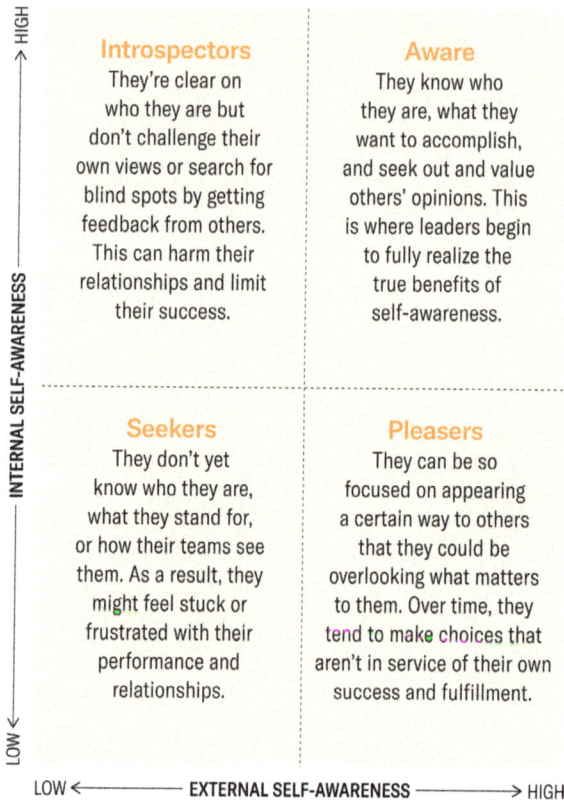

Introspectors

They're clear on who they are but don't challenge their own views or search for blind spots by getting feedback from others. This can harm their relationships and limit their success.

Aware

They know who they are, what they want to accomplish, and seek out and value others' opinions. This is where leaders begin to fully realize the true benefits of self-awareness.

Seekers

They don't yet know who they are, what they stand for, or how their teams see them. As a result, they might feel stuck or frustrated with their performance and relationships.

Pleasers

They can be so focused on appearing a certain way to others that they could be overlooking what matters to them. Over time, they tend to make choices that aren't in service of their own success and fulfillment.

INTERNAL SELF-AWARENESS (LOW → HIGH)

EXTERNAL SELF-AWARENESS (LOW → HIGH)

⏻ HBR

Figure 13: Four self-awareness archetypes

Reprinted by permission of *Harvard Business Review.* (Excerpt/Exhibit)

From "What Self-Awareness Really Is (and How to Cultivate It)" by Tasha Eurich, January 2018

As a leader, you must work on internal *and* external self-awareness. You must work on seeing yourself clearly *and* getting feedback to understand how others see you.

You can enhance your insights by asking "What?" instead of "Why?" Rather than saying, "Why do I feel so bad?" ask, "What are the situations that make me feel bad, and what do they have in common?" If you received some negative feedback from your manager, rather than ask, "Why did you say that about me?" ask, "What steps can I take to do a better job?"

"What" questions allow you to stay objective, future-focused, and empowered to act on your new insights. As Eurich states, "Leaders who focus on building both internal and external self-awareness, who seek honest feedback from loving critics, and who ask what instead of why can learn to see themselves more clearly – and reap the many rewards that increased self-knowledge delivers."[36]

Building self-regulation

Self-regulation is about reducing the intensity and frequency of negative emotions. Self-regulation makes you consciously aware of the events that prompt strong emotions within you. When you are aware, you can regulate. You can understand your emotional response and consider the consequences of that response. You are giving yourself the choice to move toward positive outcomes through your chosen responses.

If you don't regulate, you could overreact or be quick to react with an emotional outburst. If you don't regulate, you could subject yourself to negative emotions that last some time. Regulating methods include finding a distraction, taking a deep breath, and staying calm. See "Resilient, Part 1 – The Regulator."

We are in a complex world of constant change and with it brings stress. When I feel stressed, I could just shut down and go into a virtual cave, or I could run down the corridor screaming. Neither is going to look good. I recognize that we get stressed when we feel something we care about is going to be threatened. It could be a presentation to a potential client I really want to work with. It could be project deadlines that mean I have to work until late in the evening when I really want to spend time with my spouse.

I self-regulate by asking, "What am I feeling?" or " Why do I care about what I think is threatened?" When I can answer those questions, I can regulate my emotions. I can address the threat. If my presentation does not go as planned, I can reach out to the client for feedback and be in a better position as a result. If I do have to work into the evening, I will take a day off when the project is delivered and spend it at the beach with my spouse.

Building emotional control

Emotional control is a part of self-regulation. When you are mindful, you take control of your mind rather than your mind controlling you. While self-regulation reduces the intensity and frequency of negative emotions, emotional control looks to remove the triggers.

The tools you can use for self-regulation, such as breathing techniques or seeking a distraction, are good, but they are in the moment. The emotional response has already occurred. Emotional control is identifying the triggers that cause negative emotions and taking action to reduce or eliminate them. When in control, you manage an emotion's generation, experience, or expression. You can take control by avoiding stressful situations or determining how to cope with them before they occur.

For instance, I know that if I am asked to present financial information, I will get stressed. I hate financials! I know what the trigger is, and I can avoid it or cope with it. I will either ask someone else to do that part of the presentation, referring to them as far better able to articulate the findings than me, or I will find as much time as possible to rehearse the presentation, focusing on the financial part. I could also ask someone far more versed in finance to be on standby to help answer any difficult questions I may receive. When you know the triggers, you can take control.

Three core characteristics of humble leaders

Just like vulnerability is a strength, so is humility. As a humble leader, you listen to others, learn from your mistakes, and empathize with your team members. In turn, this creates an environment of trust and respect.

According to a research paper titled "Do Humble CEOs Matter? An Examination of CEO Humility and Firm Outcomes," more humble CEOs lead executive leadership teams that collaborate better, jointly make decisions, and have a greater shared vision. Humble CEOs boost the chances that executive leadership teams will adopt both exploration and exploitation strategies, and this flexibility leads to better firm performance.[37]

Humble leaders have three core characteristics:

- They have a willingness to see themselves accurately (self-awareness).
- They arc teachable.
- They have an appreciation of others' strengths and contributions.

Willingness to see oneself accurately

Self-awareness, or a willingness to see yourself accurately, means you know who you are. Understanding yourself is foundational to other leadership competencies, including self-control, empathy, collaboration, effective decision-making, and building trust.

If you are self-aware, you understand your strengths and limitations. Therefore, you can build on your strengths and work to overcome your limitations. When you know your weaknesses, you can work with others with different strengths and accept that another person may have better ideas, skills, or competencies than you do.

When you are not self-aware, you can alienate others by not understanding your impact on them. Humility is the ability to see yourself as you are.

Here are some more strategies for developing self-awareness:

- **Stop treating your feelings as good or bad.** Judging your emotions prevents you from understanding them, adds more emotions to the pile, and keeps you from seeing the cause of the original feeling. Understand, don't judge.

- **Observe the ripple effect of your emotions.** Recognize that when you act on your emotions, the results can be long term. Your emotions can affect others, and they also have physical effects on your own body. Your heart rate and breathing pace quicken, your muscles tense, and your body temperature rises.

- **Feel your emotions physically.** Learn to spot the physical changes that come with your different emotions, and you'll have a better understanding of what you're feeling.

- **Know who and what pushes your buttons.** It needs to be specific – identify the exact people, situations, and environments that trigger your emotions by rubbing you the wrong way. Make a list. It will then allow you to determine the source of your reaction to these things.

- **Watch yourself like a hawk.** Develop a more objective understanding of your behavior by taking notice of your emotions and behaviors as a situation unfolds.

- **Keep a journal about your emotions.** Because emotions are so intangible, you'll need to write things down to understand them better, identify patterns, and track progress. It will also later help you to remember your tendencies in the moment.

Teachable

A teachable leader is open to personal and organizational change. This kind of leader quickly understands that old routes are not always the best or the fastest. Conditions will change.

Humble leaders never shut the door on educating themselves. They are open to personal and organizational change. They quickly understand that old routines and sacred cows are not always the best or the fastest way to improve. A teachable leader devotes a significant amount of time to learning.

Teachability is being open to feedback and acting upon it. Great leaders are great learners. Teachable leaders are:

- **Readers.** They seek out information – from traditional print books to audio. You should read newsletters, industry journals, periodicals, and the writings of other leaders.
- **Questioners.** They ask many questions, including seeking feedback on their performance. You must ask questions because you need to keep growing.
- **Listeners.** They are active listeners. It is how you know what is going on in the hearts and minds of others.
- **Embracing of change.** A humble leader needs to discern the correct change – not just change for the sake of changing. Being open and teachable helps you develop this discernment. Humble leaders are not afraid of personal change. They embrace it. You must see change as a path to progress. Being teachable means that you embrace change as a learning opportunity.

Appreciation of others' strengths and contributions

Appreciation of others is when you recognize the success, strengths, and contributions of those around you. By being appreciative, you strive to make your team feel valued for their hard work.

There are lots of ways to acknowledge your team's successes or dedication to specific roles, tasks, and projects. You can:

- Verbalize your appreciation one-on-one or in a group setting.
- Make saying "Thank you" a habit.
- Provide opportunities for your employees to develop skills to help them achieve their personal and professional goals.
- Advocate for employees when they want to take on new work or advance within your organization. Doing so will motivate others to follow suit and create a more positive work environment!

Cognitive biases: types and tips

Mindful leaders must be aware of cognitive biases. You must know how to avoid them, and, if you succumb to them, how to overcome them. Cognitive biases are defects in your thinking. They can cause you to make bad decisions, draw wrong conclusions, and focus on the wrong things.

You must be self-aware and recognize when you may exhibit cognitive bias. You can then work to remove it and avoid it in the future. If you do not recognize it, it can be extremely dangerous to you, the team, and the organization.

According to the Cognitive Bias Codex[38], there are approximately 180 cognitive biases, and the list is frequently updated. I will now explore the ten cognitive biases I see most frequently exhibited by leaders.

Proximity bias

Proximity bias occurs when you give preferential treatment to those closest to you. It has become particularly prevalent in remote working arrangements. It is dangerous because it can create a two-tier system – those working in the office and those working remotely.

Research has shown that many employees are concerned that proximity bias will negatively impact their career progression if they work remotely. They fear that the boss (note that I'm not using the term "leader") will favor those they can see, including giving them the best assignments and projects, and putting them forward for promotion.

In a Unispace study titled "Returning For Good," which surveyed 9,500 employees and 6,650 employers from seventeen countries, eighty-four per cent of employers indicated that the chance to progress in their role would be limited for employees not in the office.[39] Another global survey, the results of which are documented in the "2023 Future of Working and Learning Report," found that seventy-one per cent of senior HR leaders and sixty-two per cent of senior business leaders agree or strongly agree that in-person workers probably benefit from a proximity bias.[40]

When some attendees join meetings remotely while others sit physically with the boss, proximity bias can become apparent. Not only does the boss favor the contributions of those in the room, but they also assign tasks to those in the room rather than a remote worker better suited to undertake the task. The deluded boss believes visible employees are more productive than invisible ones, therefore driving proximity bias, even though research indicates that remote workers are often more productive than office workers.

Proximity bias is an out-of-sight, out-of-mind mentality. The tradition of in-person employees that permeated organizations pre-pandemic has led to a managerial mindset that wants to see employees (in the same physical location), manage them, and control them. It is an ingrained mindset that must change.

Confirmation bias

Confirmation bias is the tendency to search for, interpret, favor, and recall information in a way that confirms or supports one's prior beliefs or values.

You search for information that supports your pre-existing opinion. You start with a particular viewpoint about something and then search for information that will uphold that view. Imagine you are watching your favorite sports team, and the referee makes a call that benefits your team. You believe that is a good call. When the referee makes a call against your team, you see that as a bad call. That is confirmation bias at play.

If you have ever conducted research, then you know you should read all the studies undertaken with an objective mindset. However, chances are that you have a theory about what you are researching, and confirmation bias can lead you to uncover the studies that support your theory. You may enter search terms that favor your theory, for example. You may closely examine studies supporting your theory and disregard the details in the ones that don't.

It could play out in the workplace when the CEO believes that investment in a particular ERP system will deliver the most significant benefits. The CEO gathers and directs a team to conduct market research on this system and compare it with others. The research team collects the data. The CEO's confirmation bias means he only wants to get the data from the research supporting his belief. The CEO's confirmation bias also influences the research team; they know the CEO wants a particular dataset to confirm his beliefs. It results in skewed research, giving the answers that the CEO wants.

Confirmation bias does not allow you to change your perspective and adapt your mindset to the environment. When you exhibit affinity bias (coming up next) and favor a job applicant because of it, you might display confirmation bias by posing questions that allow that individual to shine, leading to their selection for the role.

Affinity bias

Everyone has a predisposition to favor people who remind them of themselves. You may favor those who think like you, look like you, have a similar background and experiences, have the same beliefs and value system, share the same educational structure, have the same religion, share the same interests, and so on.

When applied to the workplace, this can impact the hiring process. Affinity bias can mean that you employ people who think and look like you, or went to the same school or college as you. It can influence who you recognize, reward, and promote.

Affinity bias leads you to like, associate with, and recruit people to whom you feel most similar. When you meet someone, you often unknowingly assess how different or similar they are to you. Similarity provides comfort, while differences can make you feel threatened. Some people deal with this by living in bubbles. They surround themselves with people who are like them.

The bubble will stop you from being a good leader. It results in groupthink as you surround yourself with people who think like you do. You won't hear diverse viewpoints or opinions different from yours. The like-minded people you associate with confirm what you are thinking. It is dangerous to isolate yourself from ideas different from yours and voices that will challenge your thinking. Your affinity bubble will stifle creativity and innovation. You cannot allow affinity bias to influence who you hire, recognize, promote, and reward.

Bandwagon bias

This bias is a form of groupthink. It is when you believe something because other people believe it. It stops you from thinking for yourself and being creative. It stops you from questioning or challenging. It prevents you from making sound decisions.

You adopt a certain mindset, behavior, or attitude simply because everyone else does. This is understandable. Most people want to conform, be a part of the group, and share the thoughts and ideas of others. They want to fit in. The more people who do something, the more likely others will "jump on the bandwagon."

It is important to note that bandwagon bias may not always be incorrect. What everyone else believes and is saying may be the truth. But, when the bias is wrong, it is dangerous. An example of bandwagon bias is when the executive team must make an important decision and most of the executive team is in support of one option that is on the table. Others have reservations and concerns but do not speak up because of bandwagon bias (groupthink). The decision is disastrous for the business. If questioned, it could have been avoided.

Status quo bias

Status quo bias is an emotional bias, a preference for maintaining your current or previous situation, or a preference not to undertake any action to change this current or previous state. It might become apparent when given the chance to assume a new position in a different team within your organization. You become so worried about moving to the new role that you reject the opportunity.

Status quo bias makes people resist change. They just want things to stay the way they are. It becomes more prevalent when a significant change is underway. When you have status quo bias, you will see the losses as more significant than the potential gains from a change. You will focus on what you could lose rather than how you may benefit.

Blind spot bias

This bias causes you to be less aware of your own biases than those of others, and you assume that you are less susceptible to biases than others. The danger of blind spot bias is that you fail to see the impact of biases on your judgment and decision-making.

An example of this bias playing out is when you review a conflict that has occurred in the workplace. You believe that your interpretation of it will be fair, while others' interpretations will be biased. Here's another example: you might blame a project failure on your colleagues, failing to recognize the part you had to play in the setback. When you dismiss your responsibility, you are exhibiting blind spot bias.

Recency bias

Recency bias is an unconscious tendency to consider events that happened recently or bits of information received recently to be more important than those less recent. It is an important bias for leaders to recognize, as this bias restricts them from seeing the bigger picture and considering all the information, including what has happened in the past.

It could harm performance reviews where you consider an incident that happened recently rather than the commendable track record of the employee. It can also have the reverse effect when you give a good review to an employee who performed well recently even though they have not performed well in the past.

It also impacts employees' willingness to innovate, experiment, or try something different. Despite delivering excellent outcomes over the past months, they are concerned that one mistake or setback will be what you remember rather than everything they have achieved. Their focus is staying on the right side of you instead of being creative and innovative.

Recency bias can influence decision-making. You favor recent data over long-term trends. You may be considering investment in a new technology platform and have looked at several options worth discussing. Some of them could be better than others (based on the supplier, the platform performance, the customer base, and the ability to scale), but the one encountered most recently will seem the best because of recency bias.

It can impact your perception of your performance. You may have had a great week and outperformed management expectations, but Friday was full of challenges and problems, so you feel discouraged, disappointed, and defeated at the end of the week despite the rest of the week being good. This will adversely impact your mental well-being.

Optimism bias

Optimism bias is when you overestimate your likelihood of experiencing positive outcomes and events, and underestimate your likelihood of experiencing negative events. People with this bias are sometimes quite unrealistic about what might go wrong when making a business decision. Failure could be imminent when your subjective confidence in your judgments is regularly greater than the facts suggest.

Employees may find it difficult to follow you if you always see things as having positive outcomes rather than assessing the facts. Optimism bias is when you believe you can achieve stretch targets, year on year, even though competitors are failing. You may think you can deliver a huge transformation program even though the timeframes, available resources, and current climate say otherwise. While it's important to be a leader with a "can-do" attitude, you don't want to commit to something impossible.

Conservatism bias

Conservatism bias is like affinity and confirmation bias. It is when you favor familiarity. Conservatism bias favors existing information over new information that threatens to change your preconceptions. When you get new information, you tend to value it less or dismiss it, while you give more weight to information supporting a previous belief.

You resist changing your opinion even when presented with new information. Conservatism bias means inaction. It leads to risk aversion, which is not always good. This is why Blockbuster turned down the acquisition of Netflix for fifty million dollars. The executive in charge found it easier to do nothing than take a risk.

Fundamental attribution bias

Fundamental attribution bias refers to your tendency to believe that what people do reflects who they are. It also means you attribute your behavior to external factors outside your control. You overemphasize personal characteristics and ignore situational factors when judging others' behavior. You make fast and often incorrect judgments of others without considering contributing factors.

If someone is late for a meeting, you may consider them unprofessional, even though they are rarely late and, on this occasion, they were late due to a medical emergency at home. This bias negatively impacts your relationships with others. You do not give them the benefit of the doubt, fail to see the bigger picture, and use inadequate information to make judgments.

Avoiding and overcoming cognitive biases

You can use the following tactics to avoid and overcome cognitive biases. I have pinpointed where a tactic is related to a particular bias.

1. **Practice self-awareness:** Seeing the bias is the first step to avoiding it or overcoming it. Recognition leads to remediation. You can fix it. Accept the fact that you may be susceptible to cognitive biases.

2. **Solicit feedback:** Intentionally ask others for feedback. Ask them to call it out if they think you are exhibiting a cognitive bias. The important thing is that you must act on the feedback. Encourage everyone to call it out when they observe a cognitive bias in you or one of their colleagues. Make it part of the team charter and value system.

3. **Prioritize leadership development:** Recognizing cognitive biases in yourself and others must be part of leadership development in your organization. When you accept that an unconscious bias may influence your behavior, learn to identify the bias, and implement tactics to avoid or overcome it so you can be a better leader.

4. **Learn to trust:** You must learn to trust others. You employed adults, so treat them as such. Trust them to do the right thing. It is particularly important if there is proximity bias or productivity paranoia (when you believe a person will be less productive if you cannot see them).

5. **Measure the right things:** You must measure performance on outputs, not inputs. You must measure performance based on outcomes and value-added, not hours spent at a desk. When doing this, you can avoid proximity bias because you measure outcomes regardless of an employee's location.

6. **Have regular conversations:** Regular and frequent conversations with all team members, irrespective of location, are essential. It should include a conversation about their performance as well as yours. Regular performance conversations help avoid recency, affinity, and proximity biases. Diligently record these performance conversations so you can look back at an employee's track record and not just the past week. Seek employee feedback on your performance in these conversations while ensuring you have created an environment of psychological safety so there is no fear of repercussion following the conversation. Check whether you are perceived to have a cognitive bias.

7. **Challenge others:** Get others to challenge your thinking and your decisions. Make it safe for them to do so. Make questioning decisions an inherent part of teamwork, meetings, and collaborations. Create a culture where no one ever assumes the leader's decision is correct. Get everyone to play the devil's advocate to provide debate and test the strength of an argument. It avoids or overcomes bandwagon bias, confirmation bias, conservatism bias, and status quo bias.

8. **Foster diversity and inclusion:** Intentionally invest in building a team with diverse backgrounds, experiences, capabilities, and competencies. Ensure that everyone feels included and has a sense of belonging. A diverse team helps avoid bandwagon bias, confirmation bias, recency bias, and conservatism bias. Diversity of thinking can uncover and challenge many biases.

9. **Use technology:** Use technology to reduce subjectivity and expose cognitive biases. Indeed, artificial intelligence can streamline decision-making by eliminating irrelevant data and focusing on pertinent information. It could find the best candidates for a role out of a heap of resumes without any chance of affinity bias creeping in. It can then guide you

based on what is objectively best rather than what you have done in the past (recency bias, confirmation bias, status quo bias).

10. **Be brave:** You must be brave, strong, and confident to admit you were wrong. It is not a weakness to succumb to a cognitive bias but it is a weakness not to do something about it. Admitting a mistake makes you vulnerable, but you must remember that vulnerability is not a sign of weakness but courage.

Real-world example: Mahatma Gandhi

Mahatma Gandhi[41] was a mindful leader. He used mindfulness – self-awareness, self-regulation, and emotional control – to connect with his inner self and gain clarity in his social and political activism. He was also a humble leader. Among his many famous quotes is, "Service without humility is selfishness and egotism." Gandhi always prioritized his people's needs and was quick to credit others for their contributions.

Gandhi led India's struggle for freedom. He did not follow the crowd, which blindly accepted the given system of British colonialism for centuries. He saw the injustice and he wanted change. With his strong belief in the value of humility, he effectively applied the principles of nonviolence (*ahimsa*) and nonviolent resistance (*satyagraha*) in his leadership to free India.

On March 12, 1930, he began his defiant march to the sea in protest of the British monopoly on salt. Britain's Salt Act prohibited Indians from collecting or selling salt, a staple in the Indian diet. Instead, Indians had to buy salt from the British, who had a monopoly over the manufacture and sale of salt, and imposed a heavy salt tax.

He commenced his campaign of *satyagraha* or mass civil resistance. He marched with seventy-eight followers on a 241-mile trek to the coastal town of Dandi on the Arabian Sea. On the morning of April 6, he and his followers picked up handfuls of salt along the seashore. In doing so, they technically "produced" salt and broke the law.

By this time, Gandhi was accompanied by a crowd of tens of thousands. Civil resistance soon broke out all across India, involving millions of Indians, and British authorities arrested more than 60,000 people. Gandhi himself was arrested on May 5, but the *satyagraha* continued without him. There was an international outcry against British policy in India.

Gandhi was released from prison in January 1931. British leaders acknowledged him as a force they could not ignore. The Salt March was one of the most successful campaigns in Gandhi's struggle against British rule in India. India's independence was granted in August 1947. Gandhi was assassinated less than six months later.

Adaptive

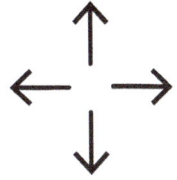

An adaptive leadership mindset is knowing what to do when you don't know what to do. Adaptive leaders learn through experimentation and manage the context, not the instruction set. They cultivate a diversity of views to generate a wealth of options. They lead with trust and respect, and provide autonomy.

I like to use the analogy of a shepherd when I describe adaptive leadership. "What does a shepherd have to do with adaptive leadership?" I hear you say. The best description comes from Pope Francis. In an address to his leadership (that is, his bishops) in November 2013, he described how shepherd leaders look after their followers:

"To do so, he will sometimes go before his people, pointing the way and keeping their hope vibrant. At other times, he will simply be in their midst with his unassuming and merciful presence. At yet other times, he will have to walk after them, helping those who lag behind and – above all – allowing the flock to strike out on new paths."[42]

Adaptive leaders lead from the front when clear direction is needed, and when uncertainty or anxiety may restrict team performance. They will lead from the core when the team needs more detail, and they need to check in on how the team and its members are faring. They will lead from the back to support those struggling, and let those upfront take the lead and explore their leadership capabilities and competencies. Adaptive leaders move between these positions with agility in response to the needs of the individual, team, and organization. They adapt to changes in the environment in which they operate.

One of my most thumbed books is *The Practice of Adaptive Leadership: Tools and Tactics for Changing Your Organization and the World*.[43] It was written by those I call the grandfathers of adaptive leadership – Ronald Heifetz, Marty Linsky, and Alexander Grashow – in 2009.

The book states, "We live in a time of danger and opportunity. Individuals, organizations, communities, and countries must continuously adapt to new realities to simply survive. Wanting more, wanting to thrive even under constantly shifting and often perilous conditions, people in all sectors are called upon to lead with the courage and skill to challenge the status quo, deploy themselves with agility, and mobilize others to step into the unknown."

This sentiment is still relevant today – perhaps even more so. The pandemic fundamentally changed how people work and disrupted many long-held beliefs regarding how people organize themselves. The next significant disruption is right around the corner. It may not be another pandemic, but, whatever it is, chances are we will not see it coming. We just have to be prepared for it.

Before we explore adaptive leadership practices, I want to explore what I believe are adaptive leaders' fundamental and foundational traits. This book discusses many of them in other chapters. The structure is deliberate, allowing you to determine which traits you need to develop to be an effective adaptive leader and how you will apply them in your organization.

Adaptive leadership traits

The following are the traits that every adaptive leader must possess.

Seeing yourself as a system

We discussed self-awareness in the previous section, but there's another idea I'd like to share with you. Self-awareness is your ability to monitor your inner and external world. It is what Heifetz, Grashow, and Linsky refer to as seeing yourself as a system:

"You are a system as complex as the one you are trying to move forward. To understand your personal system, you have to take stock of many different things: your personality, life experiences, cognitive and other skills, and emotional makeup. You also need to appreciate that your behaviors and decisions stem not just from forces within yourself as a system but also from forces acting on you in any given organizational situation."

When you see yourself as a system, you will recognize that you have more than one you. You have many identities, and how you interact and intervene will change depending on the context in which you find yourself. Your ways of being and doing may not always be consistent, depending on the situation.

You must understand this complexity, multiplicity, and inconsistency about yourself and how you interact with the larger system you are a part of. You must recognize how you change over time – who you were yesterday may not be who you are today. As the organization changes, so do you.

Adaptive leaders can diagnose themselves and the situation they find themselves in. You can evaluate yourself and manage your emotions by increasing your self-awareness. Heifetz, Grashow, and Linsky refer to this as knowing your tuning. You are like a stringed instrument, tuned differently from everyone else, and your strings resonate with your environment based on your tuning. You can respond instead of react once you understand what is pulling your strings.

Embracing a growth mindset

You need self-awareness to become an adaptive leader, but you must also possess a growth mindset – a term coined by Doctor Carol Dweck[44], an American psychologist and professor at Stanford University. She and her colleagues became interested in students' attitudes about failure. They noticed that some students rebounded while others seemed devastated by minor setbacks. After studying the behavior of thousands of children, Dr Dweck coined the terms "fixed mindset" and "growth mindset" to describe the underlying beliefs people have about learning and intelligence.

These mindsets describe how you view your intelligence and personality. Dweck wrote about these mindsets in her 2006 publication *Mindset: The New Psychology of Success*.[45] When you believe you can get smarter, you understand that the effort will make you stronger. You then put in the time and effort to achieve your goals. People with a fixed mindset believe their success is due to their innate ability. People with a growth mindset believe their success is due to hard work, learning, training, determination, and perseverance.

Fixed-mindset individuals dread failure because it is a negative statement regarding their basic abilities. In contrast, individuals with a growth mindset don't mind or fear failure as much because they understand that they can improve their performance and that failure is a source of learning. People with a growth mindset can adapt.

Here's an example that demonstrates the difference between a fixed and a growth mindset.

It's performance review time with your boss. Upon reflection, you believe you did well. However, your boss doesn't have the same opinion and thinks you have areas for self-development. You are upset. On the way home from work, you get a flat tire and have to call for roadside assistance, which takes forever to arrive and means you get home late. When you get home, you call one of your siblings to discuss your day and vent your frustration, but you feel the cold shoulder treatment, which makes your day worse.

You can consider the events of your day in two ways.

With a fixed mindset, you are likely to tell yourself:

- "I'm a failure."
- "I'm stupid."
- "I'm going nowhere."
- "I'm on my own."
- "No one cares."

With a growth mindset, you are likely to tell yourself:

- "I need to follow my boss's advice and work harder in some areas of my development."
- "I need to get my car serviced more often and align my wheels."
- "I need to learn how to change a tire myself and check my spare tire is in good condition."
- "I wonder if my sibling also had a bad day – maybe worse than mine."

The following image highlights the research carried out by Dr Dweck. It should be apparent that you will not be an adaptive leader if you are on the left-hand side of the graphic. In contrast, adaptive leaders embrace challenges, persist through setbacks, and are willing to work hard to grow. They welcome feedback and learn from others.

Adaptive leadership will take you out of your daily routine into unknown territory. It brings risk, as you cannot rely on what you learned in the past. You have to unlearn and relearn. You cannot take on an adaptive challenge (more on this shortly) without making adaptations yourself. With a growth mindset, you can embrace these challenges and grow.

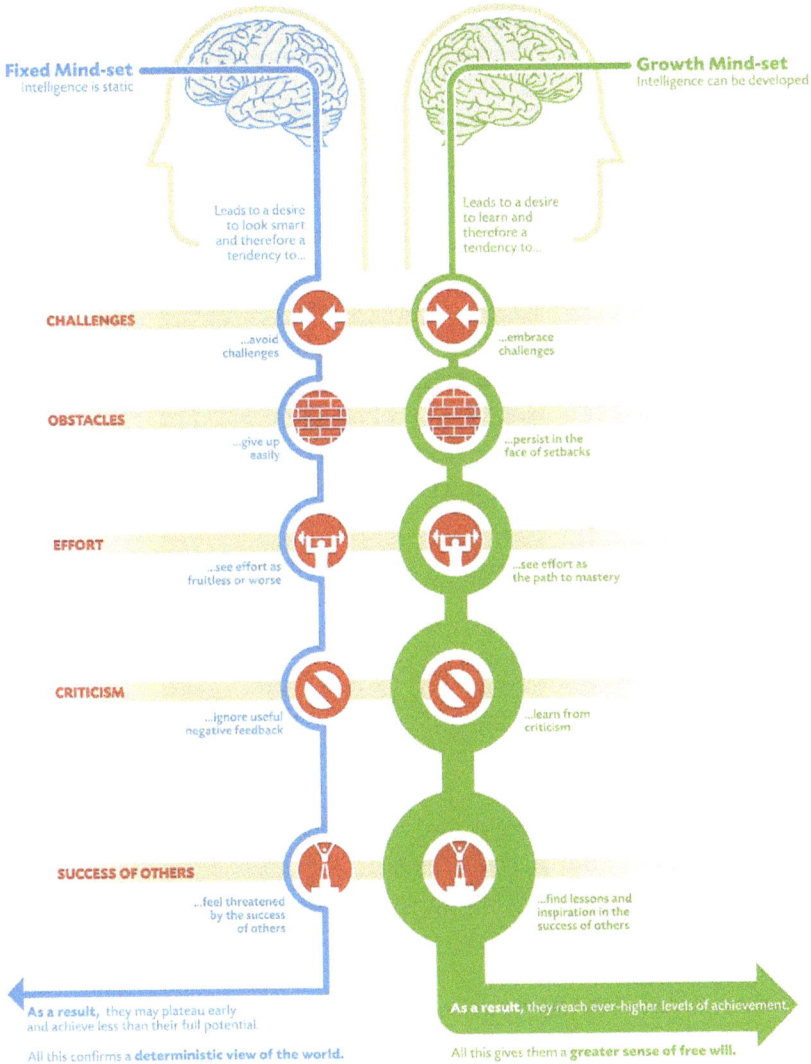

Fixed Mind-set
Intelligence is static

Growth Mind-set
Intelligence can be developed

Leads to a desire
to look smart
and therefore a
tendency to...

Leads to a desire
to learn and
therefore a
tendency to...

CHALLENGES
...avoid
challenges

...embrace
challenges

OBSTACLES
...give up
easily

...persist in the
face of setbacks

EFFORT
...see effort as
fruitless or worse

...see effort as
the path to mastery

CRITICISM
...ignore useful
negative feedback

...learn from
criticism

SUCCESS OF OTHERS
...feel threatened
by the success
of others

...find lessons and
inspiration in the
success of others

As a result, they may plateau early
and achieve less than their full potential.

All this confirms a **deterministic view of the world.**

As a result, they reach ever-higher levels of achievement.

All this gives them a **greater sense of free will.**

Figure 14: Fixed mindset versus growth mindset

Source: www.mindsetworks.com/science/Impact

Adaptive leaders have a continuous learning mindset. Here is what continuous learning looks like within an organization:

- People who make mistakes or experiment with new ways of doing things are not marginalized. They are recognized.

- When making strategic decisions, the company considers the perspective of many employees, especially those closest to the customer, consumer, or constituent.

- Planning and review sessions are regularly scheduled and include people from all levels of the organization.

- When something goes awry, it is acknowledged, assessed, and celebrated for its learning opportunity.

- Everyone is encouraged to take time out to refresh and gain new perspectives.

- Formal or informal boundaries do not hinder cross-functional communication, interaction, and collaboration.

- Reflection is encouraged on an individual and team level.

- Coaching and mentoring, as well as learning and development, are available to all employees.

- Everyone knows that plans reflect a point in time and will change as new information becomes available.

Listening and speaking from the heart

As an adaptive leader, you must be able to communicate and listen effectively. To motivate people to follow you, you must speak in a language that resonates with them and listen carefully to their responses. Heifetz, Grashow, and Linksy call this listening and speaking from the heart.

When working with a group, you must practice active listening. You must listen for clues beyond just the words spoken. What does the body language tell you? What does the intonation tell you? If you are unsure what it tells you, ask questions. Ask open-ended questions that require more than just a yes or no answer. Probe and find out what is causing anxiety or concern. What are people afraid of? What political agenda is at play? What are the conflicts?

You must also be an effective communicator by communicating openly and honestly. When you are leading people through change, it is their hearts that you must win over, not their heads. If you want them to let you into their hearts, you must let them into yours. You must speak from the heart.

Being authentic

People will not follow someone they do not trust. People want to follow "real" people who are honest, courageous, and willing to get into the midst of things when needed. They want leaders who will connect with them and understand them.

When a leader is authentic and trusted, employees are more likely to be inspired and motivated. This is crucial when leading people through adaptive change. Adaptive challenges involve values, not simply facts or logic. Addressing adaptive challenges engages people's beliefs and loyalties, which lie in their hearts, not their heads.

Authentic leaders are clear on their values, and they are true to them. People know they will do what they say. They will not compromise on their values for anything. They possess integrity. Not only do they always behave in a way that aligns with their values, but they also expect the same from their employees.

Authentic leaders are not only consistent in what they say and do but also in their emotions and behaviors. They possess the self-discipline to manage their emotions. An authentic leader does not change on a whim. Their personality and values remain steadfast in the face of change, success, failure, setbacks, or praise.

Building trust

Trust aligns closely with authenticity, and people often use the words interchangeably. But trust needs to be looked at in its own right.

Adaptive leadership is about leading people through change. It is about leading teams in new and innovative ways, which requires the leader to build and maintain trust with their team. Trust in the leader means there is a foundation upon which individuals, teams, and the organization can adjust, adapt, and thrive in the face of constant and complex change.

Trust means there is no doubt. There is no doubt about another person's intentions or capabilities. Trust is a two-way street. Leaders must show trust in their team if they expect the team to trust them.

There are lots of ways to build trust in your team. I believe these are the top five elements using the acronym TRUST:

- Transparency: No one trusts a leader who hides behind platitudes and untruths. Transparent leaders are open and honest with their people. They involve their team in decision-making and share information widely, ensuring everyone is informed and involved regardless of location.
- Relationships: The relationships you create with your team, and the relationships you encourage within the team, can make or break trust. Leaders must create a personal, positive, and consistent relationship with each team member. Trust is also contagious, so as employees watch their leader build trust, they will follow suit with their fellow employees.
- Unity: Leaders building trust bring the team together physically, virtually, or in combination for team-building

activities – ones the team has indicated interest in. Trust also comes with unity resulting from team diversity, equity, and inclusion (DE&I). Adaptive leaders leading distributed teams will find that DE&I takes on a new challenge. Leaders must ensure there is no bias or preferential treatment related to where team members work.

- Safety: When you create an environment of psychological safety, trust increases. Psychological safety means employees will not be punished or humiliated for speaking up with ideas, questions, concerns, or mistakes. Leaders also establish safety, and therefore trust, by praising publicly and correcting privately.

- Touchpoints: A leader builds trust by checking in regularly with every team member. These check-ins, also known as touchpoints, include one-on-one sessions and team meetings, both informal and formal. The key to touchpoints is to keep them regular and consistent.

Embodying leadership, not authority

Many people confuse leadership with authority. You can have a person in your organization who has a position of authority but has never led the organization through adaptive change. Others may do what they say due to that person's authority, but they would not follow them as leaders. On the flip side, you can have people in your organization who have not been given formal authority but demonstrate leadership through their behaviors and actions. They look after their colleagues and peers. You trust them and would follow them.

You do not need a rank or title to be a leader. Leadership is a characteristic, not a role. Authority is a position.

Think of authoritarian leadership and adaptive leadership as two opposite ends of the scale. The Adaptive Leader Value Model illustrates the benefits of avoiding the former and adopting the latter.

Adaptive Leadership

Navigating the Complexity

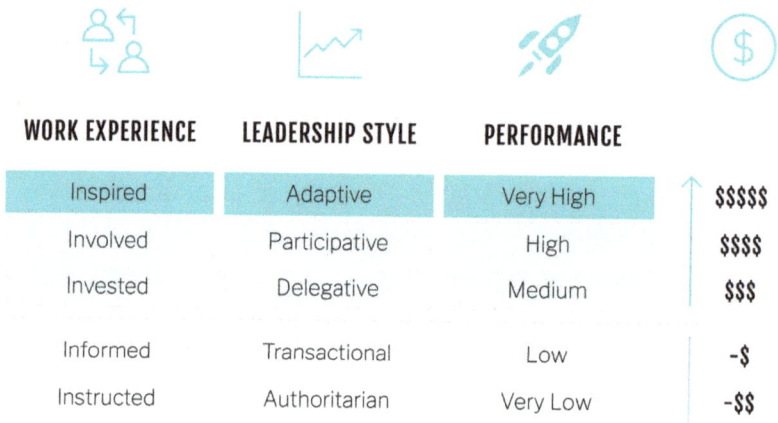

WORK EXPERIENCE	LEADERSHIP STYLE	PERFORMANCE	
Inspired	Adaptive	Very High	$$$$$
Involved	Participative	High	$$$$
Invested	Delegative	Medium	$$$
Informed	Transactional	Low	-$
Instructed	Authoritarian	Very Low	-$$

Figure 15: The Adaptive Leader Value Model

© 2024 Karen Ferris

Authoritarian and transactional leadership provides explicit instruction but creates dysfunctional environments and stifles creativity. Employees are instructed and informed, and team performance is low.

When leaders delegate and participate, employee motivation increases. Employees become invested and more involved, and performance increases.

When leaders are adaptive leaders, employees become inspired, encouraged, and empowered, and organizational performance is very high, resulting in increased profit.

Adaptive leaders must use their leadership skills instead of authority to effect change. I witnessed this a few years ago whilst consulting for a food retail organization. Isabel, a business analyst in the Business Improvement team, was very good at her job, and due to this, she was considered ideal for leading a project. She had no authority over the project team. The team's priorities aligned with those who had authority over them and their jobs. Therefore, she could not use authority to drive change.

Isabel drove change using her leadership skills. She took time to forge strong and genuine relationships with her team, gaining their support by establishing trust. She utilized her excellent communication skills to lead with clarity and her active listening skills to understand others' perspectives. She held herself accountable for her decisions and actions, and those of the team.

When you use your leadership skills, people have a choice as to whether they follow you. When you use your authority, people have little choice. They may carry out your instructions, but they are not following you. When people follow you, they do so because they feel connected to you and aligned with your goals and objectives. It is followership from the heart, not the mind. A fundamental aspect of leadership is connection; leaders do this through effective communication and active listening.

Importantly, adaptive leaders build adaptive leaders. They enable employees to anticipate what will happen, prepare for it, adapt, recover from setbacks, and keep going in the face of adversity.

Adaptive leadership in six steps

We've just discussed some of the key traits of adaptive leadership, but what does it look like in practice? In this section, I share six key steps to adaptive leadership.

At the core of adaptive leadership is distinguishing adaptive challenges from technical problems. Those with existing knowledge and expertise can implement known solutions to technical problems. For example, if your car breaks down, you call a mechanic. The mechanic may purchase replacement parts and repair the car. You may have to buy another car or you may need to hire one. Either way, there is a known solution to keep you on the road. The problem may be more complex and critical, such as replacing a faulty heart valve during cardiac surgery, but it can be addressed using existing structures, processes, and procedures.

Adaptive challenges require new, creative solutions. Often, there is a tendency to treat an adaptive challenge as a technical problem due to the personal risk in implementing new and innovative solutions. Adaptive challenges are complex and ambiguous. They may be volatile and unpredictable. Adaptive change usually requires people to learn new ways of doing things and a change in people's priorities, beliefs, habits, and loyalties.

Solutions to adaptive challenges require experiments and discoveries, which can take a long time to implement. A decree or authority cannot resolve them. Adaptive leadership entails trust, shared responsibility, and continuous learning. Adaptive challenges depend on dynamic, people-focused solutions.

With that in mind, here are the six steps that form the practice of adaptive leadership:

 Get on the balcony

 Identify the adaptive challenge

 Regulate distress

 Maintain disciplined attention

 Give the work back to the people

 Protect the voices of leadership from below

Figure 16: The practice of adaptive leadership

Get on the balcony

It is difficult to diagnose the adaptive challenge amid the action. You need to distance yourself from "on the ground" events. Heifetz, Grashow, and Linsky use the metaphor of "getting on the balcony" above the "dance floor" to get a distanced perspective and observe what is happening.

It means stepping back from the action and asking questions like:

- What is really going on here?
- What am I noticing?
- What are people saying, and what are they not saying?
- Where are the disagreements or differences?

You must get out of the fray and see the bigger picture. If you stay on the dance floor, you will only see the people dancing with and around you. You may see a very different picture when you get on the balcony. Adaptive leadership requires you to alternate between being an observer and a participant.

Imagine being on the dance floor, swept up in the music, and thinking it is a great party. You move to the balcony and note that the DJ is so loud that most people are dancing on the far side of the room. The music changes from fast to slow and back again so often that people are constantly entering or leaving the dance floor. There are many people not dancing and just hanging around by the exits. The picture you now have is one of not such a great party.

You must move back and forth from the balcony to the dance floor to continually assess what is happening in the organization and take mid-course corrective action. What may have seemed like a good plan yesterday may not look so good today.

Once you have perspective, you can identify the adaptive challenge.

Identify the adaptive challenge

We have examined how to determine a technical problem from an adaptive challenge. Each of the characteristics of an adaptive challenge is a flag or signal for diagnosis.

Heifetz, Grashow, and Linsky provide a table that connects the characteristics with a social flag, giving you a starting point for your diagnosis.[46]

Identifying a primarily adaptive challenge	
Concept	**Identifying flag**
Persistent gap between aspirations and reality	People are increasingly complaining when describing the current situation.
Responses within current repertoire inadequate	Previously successful outside experts and internal authorities unable to solve the problem.
Difficult learning required	Frustration and stress manifest. Failures more frequent than usual. Traditional problem-solving methods used repeatedly but without success.
New stakeholders need to be engaged	Rounding up the usual suspects to address the issue has not led to progress.
Longer timeframe necessary	Problem festers or reappears after short-term fix is applied.
People are starting to feel a sense of crisis	Increasing conflict and frustration lead to tension and chaos. Willingness to try something new begins to build.

When identifying adaptive challenges, you must look beyond what people say about them. Heifetz, Grashow, and Linsky call this "listening to the song beneath the words." There is so much more lurking beneath the words. It involves observing body language, eye contact, emotion, and energy. Pay as much attention to the unsaid as you do to the spoken words.

They also provide four adaptive challenge archetypes to help you identify and diagnose adaptive challenges:

- **Gap between espoused values and behaviors:**
  Organizations and individuals can have a gap between what they say they value, and how they behave. For example, there can be a gap between the organization's espoused values and actual behavior when authorities advocate collaborative behavior but reward individual performance. Closing this gap is difficult because people in the organization have been successful through their behavior patterns and will want to continue doing what has earned them success, especially when they are recognized and rewarded for doing so.

- **Competing commitments:** Often, an organization's commitments can come into conflict. When competing commitments cause conflict, organizational leaders must make a hard decision that will favor one group of people over another. In this instance, leaders often avoid making any decisions or try to find a compromise that does not serve anyone well. The conflict continues. The bottom line: hard decisions, which benefit one group of people while disadvantaging another, must be made sometimes.

- **Speaking the unspeakable:** People must share what seems unspeakable if an organization is to move forward in the face of changing priorities or external conditions. Sharing multiple perspectives can lead to adaptive solutions. For this reason, employees and leaders alike should not be afraid to share radical ideas and difficult issues, emerging conflicts, and tensions.

- **Work avoidance:** There are two common ways in which people try to avoid the potential pain of adaptive change. The first is a diversion of attention, and the second displaces responsibility. Sometimes, these may be deliberate protection against change, while at other times they may be unconscious reactions. When faced with an adaptive challenge, people may initially assess and address it realistically. But if there are no early wins, they may move into a more protective space to endure the prolonged uncertainty of complex change. Work avoidance tactics can include denying that the problem exists, applying a technical fix only, generating conflict that has no relation to the real problem, finding a scapegoat, attacking authority, or giving the problem to those who cannot do anything about it, such as consultants or committees.

Regulate distress

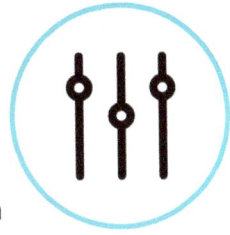

While adaptive change may be stressful for people, protecting them from it will not help. Leaders must develop workforce resilience in the face of constant and complex change. The status quo will remain if you do not address conflict related to adaptive change.

Heifetz, Grashow, and Linsky have an idea: picture yourself with your hand on a thermometer, always watching for signals that you need to raise or lower the temperature in the room. The aim is to keep the temperature – the intensity of the imbalance created by discussion of the conflict – high enough to motivate people to arrive at creative next steps and potentially useful solutions, but not so high that it drives them away or makes it impossible to function.

Leaders must help others recognize the need for change but not be overwhelmed. They must create a holding environment that enables people to unite and maintain their collective focus on what they are trying to do. The holding environment provides safety and structure for people to surface and discuss their values, perspectives, and creative ideas about challenging situations.

The temperature a group can endure will depend on their cohesiveness, shared history and values, and experience with adaptive work. A cohesive group will endure a higher temperature than a less cohesive group without breaking apart. The leader must gauge when the temperature needs to be raised or lowered.

The following table from Heifetz, Grashow, and Linsky shows how you can raise or lower the temperature in the organization.[47]

Controlling the temperature	
To raise the temperature...	To lower the temperature...
Draw attention to the tough questions.	Address the aspects of the conflict that have the most apparent and technical solutions.
Give people more responsibility than they are comfortable with.	Provide structure by breaking the problem into parts and creating timeframes, decision rules, and role assignments.
Bring conflicts to the surface.	Temporarily reclaim responsibility for the tough issues.
Tolerate provocative comments.	Employ work avoidance mechanisms such as taking a break, telling a joke or a story, or exercising.
Name and use some of the dynamics in the room to illustrate some of the group's issues. For example, getting the authority figure to do the work, scapegoating an individual, externalizing the blame, and tossing technical fixes at the situation.	Slow down the process of challenging norms and expectations.

Maintain disciplined attention

To quote Ronald Heifetz and Donald Laurie (co-authors of The Work Of Leadership), "Disciplined attention is the currency of leadership."[48]

Leaders should encourage people to focus on the challenging work they must do. Individuals and teams within the same organization often lock themselves into their way of seeing the world and acting within it. This divergence of experiences, assumptions, values, beliefs, and habits can make it difficult for people to come together and address their competing perspectives as a collective.

Paying attention to new realities and their difficulties can be challenging. People can avoid paying attention to the issues that disturb them. As discussed earlier, they can avoid facing the situation with work avoidance techniques such as diversion of attention and displacing responsibility.

Leaders must get employees to confront the rough trade-offs in values, procedures, operating styles, and power. It must occur at every level of the organization. If leaders cannot model adaptive work, the organization will fail. Leaders must be able to surface and deal with divisive issues. If they can't, they cannot expect others in the organization to do so. People must identify distractions as they occur to regain focus. Leaders must prepare to step in and help people maintain their focus.

This is an example from a telecommunications company. Marcus, the COO, noticed the relationship between his head of IT support, Pearl, and his support desk manager, Andrew, had deteriorated. Pearl had recently introduced a new process whereby every call received at the support desk required a ticket to be recorded. This affected Andrew's attitude, and he was brash and abrupt.

Marcus asked Pearl and Andrew to meet with him. He enquired about Andrew's behavior and the cause. Andrew started to blame Pearl and the reduction in the number of calls they could close in a given time. Marcus listened and then asked Pearl to explain the reasons for her process change. Pearl explained it was due to an audit and that it was a governance requirement. Andrew noted that he had not been consulted about a change in process, and Pearl admitted that she had not taken the time to involve him.

Andrew and Pearl later focused on adapting the new process to allow call resolution times to be maintained. Marcus brought the conflict out into the open, and it was used as a source of creativity. They were able to crystalize their goals and strive to achieve them by more creative means. Marcus stopped the conflict from remaining polarized and a distraction.

Give the work back to the people

Every person in the organization gains access to important information from their vantage point. Every employee needs to act on the unique knowledge that they have access to. Employees at the coalface often spot changes in customer expectations, market conditions, and competition long before their superiors do.

The over-reliance on hierarchy and the expectation that senior management will act can lead to passive behavior on the part of the employee. Leaders must learn to support their employees and operate with autonomy and trust rather than command and control. They must let employees take the initiative in defining and solving problems. Employees must learn to take responsibility.

Leaders must foster a responsibility-taking mindset across the entire organization. Here's a real-world example of an employee at the coalface spotting an opportunity before management did...

Starbucks was founded in 1971 and its mission was to be a "third place" for people to go (after their home and the office) due to its unique customer experience. In 2011, that experience was elevated when a clever barista started to write the customers' name on the cups. Head office soon found out and made the "first name" approach the standard at every store. A TV advertisement soon followed, stating, "From now on, we won't refer to you as a tall latte or a mocha, but as your folks intended – by your name. It's only a little thing. We're Starbucks. Nice to meet you."

Protect the voices of leadership from below

Everyone in the organization must have a voice if there is to be experimentation and learning. The voices routinely silenced are the deviants, creatives, and whistle-blowers. Even though they may highlight a significant problem that needs fixing, they go unheard.

Their voices may not be as articulate as others. They may be frustrated. They may be nervous or self-conscious. They may be over-zealous. All these factors contribute to the ineffectiveness of their communication. They may not pick the best place and time to voice their opinion, and they may not use the preferred communication channels.

For example, a pearl of information that needs consideration could be poorly delivered. However, ignoring it means you lose potentially valuable information and discourage a potential leader in the organization from contributing.

Leaders must create an environment of psychological safety in which every employee feels safe to share ideas, questions, concerns, or mistakes without fear of punishment or humiliation. Leaders must build teams with a shared expectation that team members will not embarrass, reject, or abuse other team members for sharing their thoughts, taking risks, or providing feedback. Everyone must keep an open mind, be aware of their biases, refrain from judgment, and actively listen to what someone says.

Real-world example: Apollo 13

In 1970, the world held its breath when it heard the now famous phrase, "Houston, we've had a problem." Apollo 13 was halfway to the Moon. An oxygen tank explosion had reduced the oxygen available to the crew – commander Jim Lovell, lunar module pilot Fred Haise, and command module pilot Jack Swigert – and had reduced power and immobilized the spacecraft.

As the command module (Odyssey) lost power, the crew moved into the lunar module (Aquarius), their lifeboat. It was a tight squeeze for the three men in a space only designed for two. The lunar module did not have enough carbon-dioxide-scrubbing chemical canisters to keep the air breathable for the crew.

So, with mission control's impromptu help, they innovated and made a crude adapter, using spare parts on board, to use the canisters intended for the command module. They called the makeshift rigging arrangement a "mailbox." It allowed them to use the command module lithium hydroxide canisters to purge carbon dioxide from the spacecraft's atmosphere.

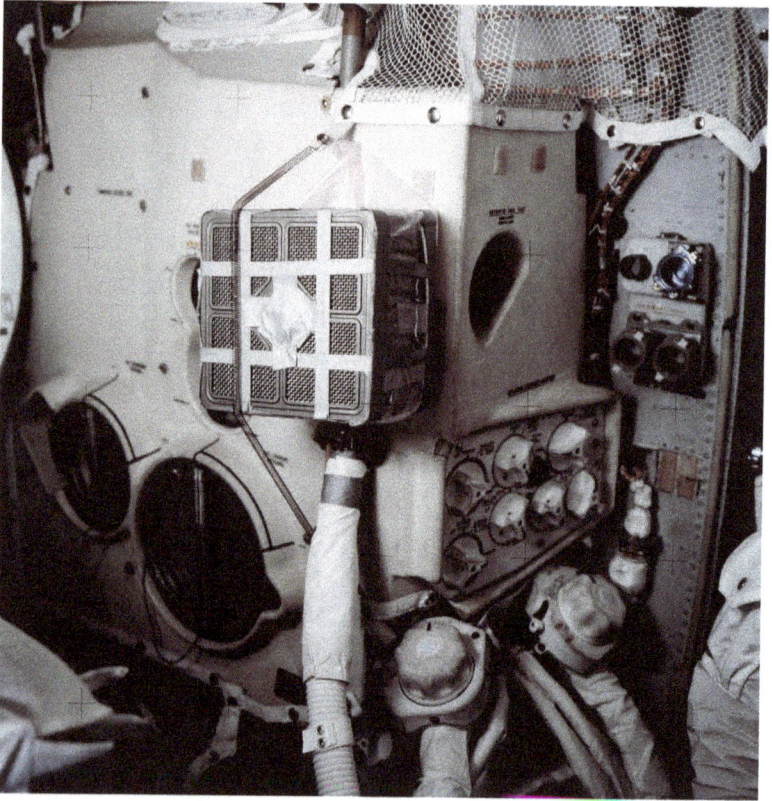

Figure 17: The "mailbox"

Source: images-assets.nasa.gov/image/as13-62-8929/as13-62-8929~orig.jpg

Navigation was a major problem. The astronauts and mission control had to work out by hand the changes in propulsion and direction needed to take the spacecraft home. The efforts NASA undertook were ones *never* undertaken before. Because Apollo 13 could not land on the Moon, the NASA ground crew had to process a series of "what if" scenarios. The scenario they decided to go with was to use the moon's gravity to return the spacecraft to Earth.

The crew used the lunar module's descent engine to modify their course to a "free-return trajectory" around the Moon, meaning lunar gravity would slingshot them back to Earth. This decision was not the result of training, a handbook, or standard operating procedures. It was the result of adaptation and adaptive leadership. The astronauts and mission control worked with the *unknown*, and they *adapted* to the situation, and the mission ended safely. Without adaptive leadership, it would have been a very different story.

Figure 18: Apollo 13 landing

Source: images-assets.nasa.gov/image/S70-35638/S70-35638~orig.jpg

Resourceful

With a resourceful mindset, you can find efficient and innovative ways to overcome problems and challenges. You are creative and determined to do whatever it takes to complete the job with what you have available. You are persistent and open-minded. You are prepared to change your approach when needed and have a growth mindset.

Resourceful leaders are productive. They know what to do, what not to do, and what to delegate. They know what resources to use, and when, for the best outcomes.

There is a tool called the Eisenhower Matrix, often called the urgent-important matrix. It helps you decide what to do by urgency and importance, and whether to delegate a task or do it at all. The name comes from its inventor – Dwight D. Eisenhower[49] – who was the thirty-fourth president of the United States, serving two terms from 1953 to 1961. He served as a US Army general and Allied forces Supreme Commander during World War II before becoming president. He was highly productive, and researchers have widely studied his methods. The Eisenhower Matrix is one of his most famous productivity tools.

Figure 19: The Eisenhower Matrix

Using the decision matrix shown here, you can categorize your actions based on four possibilities:

1. Urgent and important (tasks you will do immediately).
2. Important but not urgent (tasks you will schedule to do later).
3. Urgent but not important (tasks you will delegate to someone else).
4. Neither urgent nor important (tasks you will eliminate).

Eisenhower had a principle that differentiated urgent and important: "What is important is seldom urgent, and what is urgent is seldom important."

Urgent tasks are those you feel you *must* act on, such as making a phone call, sending a text, attending a meeting, responding to emails, and so on. They're time-sensitive in that you are working to a deadline. Examples include responding to a customer request or completing a project with an imminent due date.

Important tasks support strategic progress toward your personal and professional long-term goals. These tasks may not be urgent, but that doesn't mean they are insignificant. An example could be commencing a recruitment campaign for an executive assistant to cover a period of maternity leave.

When you can differentiate between urgent and important tasks, you can allocate them into the four quadrants of the Eisenhower Matrix:

- Do (important and urgent): These tasks are both important and urgent. They must be done as soon as possible, as they have clear consequences and impact your long-term goals. These tasks need to be done today, or tomorrow at the latest, and will be top of mind. An example could be a critical software fix for your accounting platform.

- Decide (important and not urgent): These are important but not urgent tasks. They impact your long-term goals, but you do not need to do them immediately. You can schedule them. You will address these tasks once you have completed the tasks in the "Do" quadrant.

- Delegate (not important and urgent): These tasks are not important, but they are urgent. They have an immediacy but do not impact your long-term goals. You don't need a unique skill set for these tasks, meaning you can delegate them to people with the bandwidth to handle them quickly, allowing you to focus on other things. You may also be able to automate some of these tasks. An example could be using a news aggregator rather than trawling through online sources.

- **Delete** (not important and not urgent): These tasks are not important, nor are they urgent. They do not help you meet your long-term goals. When you have allocated tasks into the other three quadrants, what is left over will likely be placed here. These tasks simply get in the way of you getting things done. Examples could be checking social media or sorting through junk mail. Often, these tasks are the ones you need to learn to say "no" to, so you don't get inundated with tasks that do not add any value.

In the next section, we'll take a closer look at the third quadrant, "Delegate," as this can be an area where many leaders come unstuck.

The art of delegation

Tasks that fall into the "urgent and not important" quadrant – Delegate – are nearly always the interruptions from your intended course of direction. The problem is that most people spend their time in this quadrant, thinking they are working on urgent tasks that are important to them when, in reality, these tasks are doing nothing to move you toward your long-term goals.

Often, tasks get stuck here because people are not comfortable with delegation. As a result, I thought I would share some key steps required for delegation to be effective.

Focus on clarity

You must be clear about the task you intend to delegate and why you are delegating it. If you are unclear before you delegate, the recipient will not be clear. That is like providing vague directions to navigate through a fog!

What outcomes do you want? When do you want them? What resources are available? How often do you want a progress update?

Consider the potential recipients of the task and whether the task may need to be broken up into smaller chunks so as not to overwhelm the recipient(s). Does the recipient have the right skills and capabilities to undertake the task without being sent into the terror zone? Putting someone into the stretch zone with the proper support and guidance is okay, but not the terror zone. That is when you burn someone out.

Assign the task

You can assign the task once you are clear and have a delegate. The person to whom you are delegating the task must know why you are doing it and why you are giving it to them.

It is paramount to start with "why." Often, because *you* are clear on why you want to delegate a task, you start with "what" and "how." For example, you might say, "I would like you to write the monthly team performance report. You can use the project progress reports, the RAID (risks, assumptions, issues, dependencies) chart, and the team engagement results. Put it in PowerPoint so we can show it at the monthly management meeting." You have stated what and how you want it delivered, but not why you are asking.

You must start with why you need the task done and why you think the delegate is the best person to undertake the task. You could say, "I have noticed you are great at collating information, distilling it, and presenting it in a digestible format. I would love it if you could produce the monthly team performance report." In this instance, you've explained to the person the reasons for their selection, ensuring they understand that you didn't assign the task to avoid doing it yourself.

Convey your requirements

When you convey your requirements, you should be clear about the task. The delegate must be clear on the desired outcomes, the timeframe, and the resources available to them. You must also contextualize the delegation not as an instruction but as a request for help.

It is an absolute motivator when you say, "I am struggling to get this month's report ready for the management meeting. Could you help me with this?" or "Your report writing skills are much better than mine. Could you assist me with this month's report?"

Ensure the delegate understands the task by getting them to repeat what they have heard. It allows you to clarify if there has been a misunderstanding. Nothing is more demotivating and demoralizing than being given a task you believed you understood and delivering something that does not yield the outcomes your leader expected. Not only will you be disappointed, but so will your delegate, and you will now have created a fear in them that if you were to delegate again, they would get it wrong. You must ensure you are both on the same page before the delegation commences.

Set clear expectations

You must make your expectations clear. Once again, there is no room for ambiguity. What sort of progress reporting do you want? How often? Do you want a regular check-in, and, if so, how often?

Your expectations regarding the outcome must also be clear. You need a management report that includes results and conclusions in a succinct way, rather than all the details behind the results. Visuals are better than words, so you want your delegate to use illustrations, graphs, and tables where possible.

Setting expectations is a balancing act because you want to avoid being prescriptive and give your delegate the chance to be creative and have some control over the outcome. You should aim to give sufficient guidance to ensure your expectations are met, while only dictating certain steps to achieve those expectations.

Offer support

Delegation is not management by abdication. When you delegate, you are giving someone else the responsibility for delivering, but you are still in the loop, so you know what is happening and whether you need to get involved. When you abdicate, you give someone responsibility, but then you disappear – you turn your back. The person is on their own.

Your delegate must know you are there to support them whenever needed. They are not on their own. You have their back. They can come to you whenever they need to.

Being decisive, yet open-minded

Resourceful leaders do not procrastinate. They are decisive. Decision-making must be well-informed and time-sensitive. You need to collect as much data and information as possible within the available time before making a decision. You must utilize your team and colleagues' knowledge, experience, and insights.

You might not have all the information you would like before you make the decision, so you must be able to gather the critical information and act on it. It also works the other way. You may not have to make an immediate decision. Still, you do not want to fall into the trap of endlessly gathering and analyzing data, and procrastinating over your decision. While your decision may not be time-bound, people are still waiting on it so they can act. An indecisive leader is frustrating, demoralizing, and demotivating.

When you are *formulating* a decision, you must get others to challenge your thinking, and you must be open to new ideas and counterarguments. More on this in just a minute.

When you *make* a decision, it must be with clarity, and it must be final. When I say "final," I mean that it is clear to those around you that you have made your decision and will act on it. There is no room for "ifs" or "buts" or "maybes." When you make a decision, you do so with confidence.

It doesn't mean that if your decision turns out to be misinformed or misdirected, you are not prepared to admit you made a mistake and change direction. It is a humble, honest, and adaptive leader who admits a mistake and sees it as a learning opportunity.

While decisiveness is crucial, it's also important for resourceful leaders to be open-minded. When you are open-minded, you are prepared to adjust your thinking when you receive new information. You see things from diverse perspectives, and you practice adaptive leadership. You are open to new ideas.

When you are open-minded, you possess a growth mindset. You have a thirst for learning. As a result, you're more likely to foster a culture of creativity, innovation, and diversity of thinking. When presented with alternative ideas and opinions, you are prepared to change your mind.

As George Bernard Shaw said, "Those who cannot change their minds cannot change anything."[50]

Part of being open-minded is doing whatever it takes to get the job done with the available resources. Resourcefulness is more than how much money is available; it is how to do the best with what is available. The resourceful leader looks for cost efficiencies through optimization and automation.

Resourcefulness means looking to innovation to find new and better ways of operating. Leaders ask, "What do we need, what is possible, what will it take, and where can we find it?" They ask, "What have we got today? What is the best we can do with it?" They are the unrelenting challengers, always asking, "How can we do better with what we have or can get?"

Real-world example: Steve Jobs and Steve Wozniak

The duo of Steve Jobs[51] and Steve Wozniak[52] – the founders of Apple Computer Company – are an excellent example of resourcefulness. They had a vision and were willing to put in the work over the long haul.

They had a product, a plan, and 1,300 dollars in capital from Wozniak pawning an HP calculator and Jobs selling his VW bus. They had thirty days to deliver on a 25,000-dollar order they fulfilled in the garage of Jobs' parents' home. All available people hand-assembled the PC kits, while Jobs and Wozniak handled the marketing and selling.

They wanted to make computers that were affordable and user-friendly. They sold the Apple 1 without a monitor, keyboard, or casing in 1976. They added a casing in 1977 with the Apple II. The Apple II revolutionized the computer industry as it could display color graphics. Sales jumped from 7.8 million dollars in 1978 to 117 million dollars in 1980 when Apple went public.

Known

(TM)

What are you known for? What do you want to be known for? The answers to those two questions are at the core of your leadership brand.

Your leadership brand is what makes you distinctive. It is your reputation. It is not only based on what you do but also on how you do it. It tells people who you are, what your values and beliefs are, and the worth that you bring. It should reflect what you are passionate about.

It showcases your character and your competencies. People know what to expect from you and what differentiates you. Your brand is what makes you unique. When you have a strong brand, people know what you are capable of and can utilize your offerings more effectively. In other words, you're more likely to attract the right people to work with and get more of the work you like to do.

In contrast, you can go unseen when people are unsure what you are known for. You want to stand out from the crowd. With that in mind, this section of the book is all about building your brand as a leader.

Creating your leadership brand

You can use these steps to create or reassess your leadership brand.

Self-assessment

Ask yourself these questions and write down your answers:

- **What are your values?** These are the things that guide the way you live and work. They are your most basic and fundamental beliefs. They define what you stand for personally and professionally. They will govern how you act and speak. They guide your decision-making. Your values must be representative of how you want to lead.

- **What are your competencies?** Identify your strengths. What are you good at? Where can you make a difference? What is your unique value proposition (UVP)? This statement clearly describes the benefits of what you can do, how you can solve problems and overcome challenges, and what makes you unique from other leaders.

- **What are you passionate about?** These are the things that motivate and excite you. They make you jump out of bed in the morning. These are the things you want to know more about. Why are you a leader?

Others' assessments

How other people see you is your current brand. Assess how other people perceive you. Get feedback from your team members and colleagues regarding your communication, knowledge-sharing, problem-solving, delegation, and decision-making styles. Determine what others see as your strengths and weaknesses.

Make a note of common terms and phrases emerging to describe you. Determine whether the perception of others aligns with your self-assessment of your values and competencies, and where you may need to work on positioning.

Your brand statement

You have collected all the information you need to create your leadership brand statement. There are no hard and fast rules, but your statement must be concise and to the point. Here is how I came up with my brand statement...

After completing the self-assessment exercise and getting feedback from others, I had the following information:

- Values: honesty, integrity, transparency.
- Competencies: pragmatism, challenging the status quo, new ways of thinking.
- Passions: developing leaders, building resilient workforces, organizational change at speed.

I then took that information and honed it into three sentences. This is my brand statement:

"I am an organizational change management rebel *with* a cause. I value honesty, integrity, and transparency, and have a pragmatic approach.

I push the boundaries to explore and develop new approaches guaranteed to improve things for all.

I am known for building leadership capability, workforce resilience, and enabling rapid organizational change."

Building trust in your brand

Trustworthiness must be at the core of your brand. We talked about how to build trust in an earlier section of the book.

There are two principal components of trust: character and competence. Richard Barrett (Founder of the Barrett Values Centre) created this model based on the Four Cores of Credibility as outlined in Stephen M. R. Covey's book *The Speed of Trust*.[53]

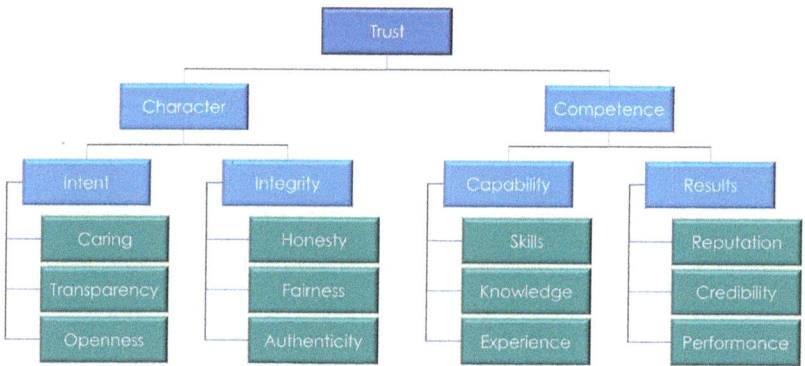

Figure 20: Trust model based on Stephen M. R. Covey's The Speed of Trust
Reproduced with permission by Richard Barrett

Character reflects how you are on the inside, including your intent and the level of integrity you display in your relationships with others. Your level of emotional and social intelligence has a huge impact in this regard. You demonstrate intent through caring, transparency, and openness; you demonstrate integrity through honesty, fairness, and authenticity.

Competence reflects how you are on the outside, including your capability and the results you deliver. This depends primarily on your mental intelligence, your education, and what you have learned during your professional career. Skills, knowledge, and experience demonstrate capability. You demonstrate results through reputation, credibility, and performance.

Both dimensions are vital, so let's discuss them in a little more detail.

Character

Character is important because a person may be competent, with great skills and capabilities, and deliver consistently, but you won't trust them if they are not honest. As you know, the key components of character are intent and integrity.

Intent

What is your motive and agenda, and how does that play out in your behavior?

Caring

Your prime intent should be caring for others. You must lead with empathy. We all live in a constantly changing, uncertain, and disruptive world. We all have different experiences, perspectives, needs, aspirations, values, and beliefs. As a leader, you must genuinely care about your team, and look out for their physical and mental well-being.

When you care, you try and see situations through the eyes of others. You can put yourself in another person's shoes. You must continually ask, "Are you okay?" or "Is everything okay?" You must be a good listener, allowing the other person to speak without constant interruption. You focus on what the person is saying and avoid distractions. You are impartial and non-judgmental. You disregard the notion of right or wrong in the discussion.

Transparency

Fostering trust means there is transparency in what you say and do. You must share information. You need to be open and honest. When you do this, it tells employees you trust them with the truth. People often intuitively know when you keep information from them, which infers you don't trust them. With transparency comes trust and respect. Being transparent is perhaps one of the most challenging areas for many leaders. When leaders learn to be transparent, it means they must trust their employees with the truth. For many, this can be a giant leap of faith.

Transparency also means you share your own mistakes and challenges with your employees. It is when you dare to be vulnerable and admit that you messed up or got it wrong. It is when you say, "I don't know the answer to that right now." When you are transparent, others will be the same. They will share shortcomings, mistakes, and setbacks. It is far more powerful than hiding them.

Openness

When you are open, you are more approachable as a leader. Employees are more likely to share information with you. It also requires an environment of psychological safety where employees feel safe to speak up, ask questions, challenge decisions, or raise concerns. When you actively listen to what they say, without judgment or bias, your employees will know that you are genuinely open to hearing their thoughts.

If there is a fear of speaking up, employees will not answer your questions honestly, which could be extremely dangerous. You need to know when a decision is wrong, when a course of direction needs to be changed, or when a problem needs addressing. Silence is deadly.

Integrity

When we talk about integrity, most people immediately think it means honesty. It does, but it also means following through on your commitments, standing by your values and beliefs, and being authentic.

Honesty

You will be seen as having integrity when you are genuinely honest in all your interactions with others. When you are honest, there is a greater chance that your employees will be honest too. Honesty builds trust and respect. When you are honest, you admit your mistakes and encourage others to do the same. It is less likely that your employees will cover up mistakes, which could turn into big problems if not addressed. Honesty means you hold yourself accountable and are authentic and transparent.

Fairness

You must be fair in your dealings with other people. You must treat everyone equally. Everyone must have the same opportunity to grow, contribute, and develop.

The fair leader must be conscious of their baggage and biases. Your baggage comprises intangible things such as feelings, circumstances, and beliefs. They are the influences and experiences you have had growing up. They can impact how you perceive others based on race, gender, sexual orientation, wealth, education, religion, and many other factors. You can learn to recognize that stereotypes are not valid indicators of another person's personality, capabilities, competencies, and so on.

You could fall victim to many biases, which we looked at in "Mindful." When you know your biases, you can implement strategies to overcome them. You must be self-aware and vigilant to recognize when a bias impacts your leadership.

Authenticity

Being your authentic self is when everything you do aligns with your goals, values, and beliefs. When you are authentic, you live your values and stand behind them. These values are the core beliefs and principles you live by personally and professionally. They guide your actions and act as a moral compass.

When you are authentic and stand by your values, you know leadership is not about always being popular. You will tackle issues you know need resolving, even though you may make enemies in the process. You will defend the decisions you make. You will call out unacceptable behavior. You will have zero tolerance for objectionable conduct that others choose to ignore.

When you live by your values, you will earn the respect of your colleagues and your team. Others will find you easier to understand. They are clear about what you want and expect from them. They know that what they see is what they get and trust you as a result.

Competence

Competence is essential because you might think a person has character, meaning they are sincere, even honest, but you won't trust that person fully if he or she doesn't get results.

Capability

Capabilities are increasingly important when the speed of change eliminates the need for certain skill sets and introduces the need for new ones at a rate never known. Skills, knowledge, and experience demonstrate capability.

Skills

Skills are the things you can do well. A leader may have integrity and intent, but they will not have credibility unless they have the right leadership skills. You must continually evaluate your skills and determine new skills you may need to acquire.

In the wake of the pandemic, many leaders have had to develop new skills to lead a distributed team, for example. Many have refused to do this. Others will not trust them if they are unprepared to acquire the skills they need to be a good leader *today*. When you acknowledge that you need new skills, and work hard to learn and develop them for the benefit of others, you will establish trust.

You must be skilled at building and maintaining good relationships with other people. You must have good conflict-resolution skills. You must be able to give feedback in a manner helpful to the recipient.

Knowledge

Knowledge is your learning, insight, and awareness. Just like skills, you must continually work to increase your knowledge. You must have a growth mindset, as we discussed earlier. With this mindset, you see opportunities instead of obstacles and are prepared to step outside your comfort zone to grow and develop.

A leader's knowledge must be contemporary. Knowledge, like food, has a shelf life. What was relevant five years ago may no longer be relevant today. And expired knowledge, like expired food, is dangerous. The wrong knowledge can lead to you making the wrong decisions, bad judgments, and big mistakes.

When you learn-unlearn-relearn, you will have the trust of others.

Experience

People will trust you when you can demonstrate a depth of experience. They trust that your experience will mean you can use good judgment when making decisions.

When you share your experiences, both the good and the bad, you are transparent and have the courage to be vulnerable. You will establish trust when you are prepared to talk about an experience where you didn't get it right the first time and made a mistake. You enable and develop others when you share your experience and expertise.

Results

Results matter to your credibility. You could have great capabilities, but without results they mean nothing. You must show that you use your capabilities to create results for others. Otherwise, there is no trust. You demonstrate results through reputation, credibility, and performance.

Reputation

Reputation means being trustworthy, but reputation is also a tool for building *more* trust. Reputation results from everything you do – what you say, how you behave, what you deliver, and your values and beliefs. Reputation is your way of being. It is your authenticity.

Like trust, when your reputation gets damaged, it can take a long time to repair. Therefore, you must work to build and maintain a good reputation. At the foundation of a good reputation is competence – you must be good at what you do – and character – you must do the right things. You can share how you are delivering great results for others without sounding arrogant. Your results also need to be delivered consistently to solidify your reputation. Reputation is your track record, not a one-off win.

Credibility

You build up credibility over time. When you are credible, your employees will trust you. They will listen to your ideas, and respect your expertise and experience. They will take you seriously. Employees will judge your credibility based on your character, competence, and caring.

You earn credibility by backing up your words with underlying knowledge and experience. You can increase your credibility by increasing your knowledge and experience, and demonstrating your competence in utilizing it effectively.

Performance

Your employees will assess your performance based on past, current, and future performance. Once again, this track record requires consistency in achieving results.

Your past performance is your reputation and track record for delivering results, not just actions. Your current performance is the results you are delivering now. Based on past and current results, your future performance is how others anticipate you will perform.

Real-world examples: Brené Brown, Gary Vaynerchuk, and Tim Ferriss

Here are the elevator pitches of some well-known and highly successful leadership brands. They are clear, concise, and benefit-driven.

Brené Brown[54]

- **Values:** courage, vulnerability, and empathy.
- **Competencies:** research, storytelling, public speaking. Translation of complex psychological concepts into accessible and relatable content.
- **Passions:** exploration of vulnerability, courage, shame, and empathy.
- **Brand statement:** Keeping it awkward, brave, and kind.

Gary Vaynerchuk[55]

- **Values:** hard work, empathy, and patience.
- **Competencies:** digital marketing, brand building, entrepreneurship.
- **Passions**: hard work, entrepreneurship, and seizing the digital age's opportunities.
- **Brand statement**: Legacy is greater than currency.

Tim Ferriss[56]

- **Values:** continuous learning, efficiency, and self-improvement.
- **Competencies:** writing, public speaking, and lifestyle experimentation.

- **Passions:** experimentation, curiosity, and optimizing every aspect of life.
- **Brand statement:** Deconstructing excellence to help you live your best life.

Accountable

Accountability is when you take responsibility for your actions. Accountability is when you do what you said you were going to do. You take ownership and follow through. Everyone in the organization, including you, must be held accountable for getting the job done. To quote the French playwright Molière, "It is not only what we do, but also what we do not do, for which we are accountable."

When you are accountable, you admit your mistakes. You take accountability when things do not go according to plan. You see these events as learning opportunities and take measures to avoid them happening again. You communicate honestly with your team about what went wrong rather than hiding the truth. When there is accountability, there is no blame game – a toxic culture in which everyone blames everyone else for mistakes.

Unfortunately, there is a big problem with accountability in the workplace. Accountability receives more lip service than action. You can see a lack of accountability when leaders and employees look one way while pointing the finger in another direction. This indicates there is a blame culture.

When there is a lack of accountability, it can have devastating consequences, including:

- **Low morale:** Without accountability, there is no motivation to perform at your best. If you are not accountable, why would you work hard to deliver outcomes that provide value? When there is a lack of enthusiasm, there is low morale. Apathy reigns.

- **Low productivity:** When there is low morale, there is low productivity. A lack of accountability means there is no incentive to meet deadlines. You disengage, and your productivity deteriorates.

- **Poor quality of work:** When employees are disengaged, it impacts the quality of work. If you are not held accountable for delivering quality outcomes, why would you check your work and take corrective action when you detect errors? If you work in a toxic environment and always watch your back, you will be distracted, leading to more mistakes.

- **Smoldering mistakes:** People brush mistakes under the carpet, hoping they will go unnoticed or someone else will take the blame. It is dangerous. If these mistakes are left uncorrected, they could manifest themselves in ways that have a damaging and long-term effect on the organization.

- **The blame game:** When there is no accountability, everyone blames everyone else for mistakes. As a leader, you may never know who was responsible for a particular action. You may end up penalizing or rewarding employees who had nothing to do with the success or failure of specific outcomes.

- **Higher turnover:** The blame game leads to a toxic culture. No one admits mistakes, and they look to blame others. There is mistrust and despair. Employees will start to leave in droves.

- **Cost:** Of course, all of these factors have a cost. There is a cost to the organization in decreased efficiency and productivity. There will be a cost in increased sick leave, absenteeism, and presenteeism. There is a financial penalty for increased turnover. There is also a cost to the individual with increased stress, anxiety, depression, and other mental health concerns.

Thankfully, there are steps you can take to create a culture of accountability in your team and organization more broadly. I will share these with you shortly. But first, I want you to take stock of your team's current level of accountability, so you have a better understanding of how much work needs to be done.

The accountability ladder: Where do you sit?

The accountability ladder is a tool to identify your level of accountability and that of your team. Bruce Gordon[57] created it when he was president of the National Association for the Advancement of Colored People (NAACP). Gordon's framework has many variations, and this one is mine.

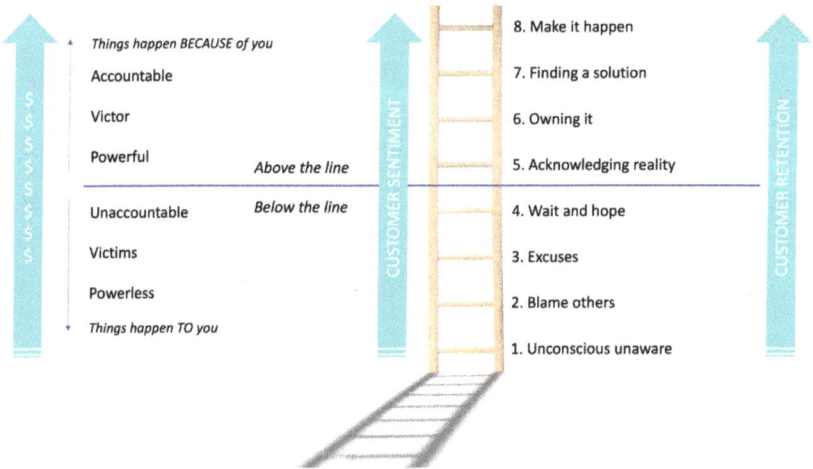

Figure 21: The accountability ladder, based on Bruce S. Gordon's 2007 framework

The ladder has eight rungs. The bottom four (below the line) represent those who are not accountable. They are victims and therefore powerless. These rungs protect their comfort zone. The accountable people are on the top four rungs of the ladder. They are victors, and therefore powerful. Here is some of the language people on each rung might use:

1. Unconscious unaware – "I didn't know."
2. Blame others – "No one told me."

3. Excuses – "Well, it's too late. There's nothing I can do about it now."

4. Wait and hope – "Maybe it will work out?"

Victims are people who don't know there is a problem. Or, if they do know a problem exists, they blame it on someone else. They make excuses, and wait and hope that things will sort themselves out. This is a victim mentality. Compare this to:

5. Acknowledging reality – "I know I should have done it. I messed up. I missed the deadline."

6. Owning it – "So, this is what I am going to do. I will take care of it – this is on me. It is my responsibility regardless of whether anyone helps me or not."

7. Finding a solution – "I have time – I can do this. Here is what I can do."

8. Make it happen – "I'm on it. Powerful people make it happen."

When you are below the line, things happen *to* you. When you are above the line, things happen *because* of you. When you and your team demonstrate accountability, customer sentiment and satisfaction increase, leading to customer retention. This increases profitability.

We can take a more in-depth look at the ladder.

8. Make it happen — The people here are all "on board." They are accountable for implementing a solution and committed to success. Goals are now accomplished.

7. Finding a solution — People here own the problem and own the solution. Actively seek to implement solutions, and even if they cannot directly do it, they will move those who can. They still OWN it.

6. Owning it — People here own the problem and honor their commitments and responsibilities. They no longer make excuses or blame others.

5. Acknowledging reality — People here have let go of magical thinking and acknowledge the reality of circumstances or events. Realization that there are tasks to be done and they are responsible.

4. Wait and hope — People here know there is a problem, but they will wait and hope for magic to happen rather than act. You must put a solution into action. Ask for help.

3. Excuses — The "I can't" stage. People here avoid responsibility by claiming confusion or incompetence. Worst attribute. Stop making excuses and get it done!

2. Blame others — Deny responsibility and shift blame to others. Moving up from this step requires you to point the finger at yourself and admit you may, in fact, be the problem, not other people or factors.

1. Unaware or unconscious — Denial – pretend there is no problem. Unaware – you do not know what or how to do it. External intervention is likely to be needed.

Figure 22: The accountability ladder deep dive, based on Bruce S. Gordon's 2007 framework

You can use the accountability ladder in one-on-one meetings or team meetings.

You could use it one-on-one to discuss where your employee sees themselves on the ladder and where you see them. If there are differences, you can explore why that might be and how your employee can get to the rung you would like them to aim for. If there is agreement, you can explore how your employee can move up the ladder or maintain their current position.

You can use it in team meetings to get the team to think about where they are on the ladder. You can help the team determine how to improve or sustain their current position.

Creating a culture of accountability

The proper steps can create a workplace accountability culture. This will drive organizational success through increased employee engagement and motivation, which in turn boosts performance and productivity. Everyone can foster a culture of accountability by accepting responsibility before anyone assigns blame.

ACCOUNTABILITY	SYMPTOM	PERFORMANCE	
Very high	Accomplishment	Engagement	$$$$$
High	Ownership	Motivation	$$$$
Medium	Acknowledgment	Trust and support	$$$
Low	Excuses	Unproductive	-$
Very low	Denial	Low morale	-$$

Figure 23: The Accountability Value Model

© 2024 Karen Ferris

The Accountability Value Model illustrates what happens in the organization as accountability increases...

- When accountability is very low, there is denial that there is a problem, resulting in low morale.
- Low accountability leads people to make excuses and blame others. Everyone avoids responsibility by claiming confusion or incompetence, and productivity declines.
- Accountability increases when everyone acknowledges a problem and lets go of the hope that the problem will

disappear. They realize that they are a part of the solution. This acknowledgment fosters trust and support across teams.

- High accountability happens when people take ownership of a problem and its solution. They are committed to delivering outcomes with business benefits. They are motivated and honor their commitments and responsibilities.

- Very high accountability results in a shared sense of accomplishment and increased employee engagement. Employees here are all on board. Goals are achieved.

Ultimately, accountability improves employee performance and boosts the bottom line. Here are some suggestions for creating a strong culture of accountability in your organization.

Start at the top

Accountability starts at the top. It begins with leaders (you). If you don't hold yourself accountable, you cannot expect others to be accountable for delivering outcomes, meeting deadlines, accurate reporting, and so on. When you hold yourself accountable, your employees will follow suit.

Set clear expectations

To hold yourself and others accountable, you must set clear expectations. You must know what you expect of yourself, and others must know what to expect of you. In addition, everyone needs to know what is expected of them. You cannot hold someone accountable for something they know nothing or little about.

What is the outcome you are looking for? What are the timeframes? How will you measure success? Make sure your employees understand your expectations. It is a two-way conversation. Your employees should have autonomy over how they will achieve the desired outcome, and they should discuss this with you. At the end of the conversation, get your employees to explain the outcome they will deliver, the timeframe, how they will achieve it, and how you will measure success. It ensures you are both on the same page and there is alignment.

Have a sense of purpose

Everyone must have a sense of purpose. It is hard to be accountable for something if you do not know why you are doing it. How is what you are doing aligned with the goals of the organization? Being accountable for delivering something makes sense when you have a sense of purpose. It's okay to tell someone what you want them to do, but you must start with the why. Revisit "Resourceful" for a refresher on this.

Measure performance transparently

Everyone must know how performance and success are going to be measured. There cannot be any surprises. You must discuss it during the expectations conversation. Have regular milestone check-in meetings. I suggest these take place every week. Set weekly milestones that have clear, measurable targets. You must not wait until an assignment's end to determine whether your employee has met the outcomes. This is setting you both up for failure. Don't just assume that your employees will seek help if they struggle. Provide the opportunity in the regular meetings. You can immediately address the situation if the weekly target is not met. You should work together to get things back on track.

Communicate, communicate, communicate

Communication is key to accountability. It must include two-way feedback on what went well and what didn't. It should look at the team's performance and your performance. Regular communication must reinforce the culture of accountability within the organization. Communication should ensure everyone understands what accountability means.

Call it in

Everyone must be able to call it in when others are not doing what they said they would. There is a distinct difference between call-in and call-out. A call-out is to bring attention to something publicly. A call-in initiates a one-on-one conversation to make another person aware of their behavior.

The team charter should state that everyone can call it in if they observe someone not being accountable. Many factors may be at play in impacting a person's accountability, so you must listen to what they say and help them where you can. You must be timely and specific. You should initiate the conversation immediately after observing the behavior and describe what you witnessed. Do not be personal. It is about behavior, not the person.

Highlight the power of choice

We often hear accountability talked about in terms of consequences. When this happens, people fear being held accountable due to the implied punishment. Accountability is about having a choice to take ownership. There is always a choice. If an employee chooses not to be accountable, have a conversation about their choice and the natural consequences of that choice.

As a leader, you must trust that everyone in your team will take ownership of their behavior, performance, and outcomes. When it doesn't happen, you discuss their freedom of choice and responsibilities. You act as a coach to support them.

Real-world example: Harry S. Truman

US President Harry S. Truman possessed the leadership qualities of integrity and accountability. He became president in 1945. During his two terms, he made many decisions in what were some of the toughest times in US history.

He ordered the atomic bombs dropped on Japan in 1945, with the aim of destroying Japan's ability to pursue war. The American soldiers and civilians were tired from four years of war. At the time, American forces occupied Okinawa and Iwo Jima, and were intensely fire-bombing Japanese cities. But Japan had an army of two million strong stationed in the home islands, guarding against invasion. Japanese surrender was not on the horizon.

President Truman made what would be the most difficult decision of his life. On August 6, 1945, an atomic bomb was dropped on Hiroshima, vaporizing between 70,000 and 126,000 Japanese citizens. On August 9, a second bomb was dropped on Nagasaki, and 80,000 Japanese people died. The Japanese surrendered on August 14, 1945.

Truman believed that the decision was purely military and that the bombs saved Japanese lives as well. Prolonging the war was not an option for him. While the bombs did end the war, it was seen by many as an unnecessary barbaric act and a war crime, killing as many as 226,000 people, most of whom were civilians.

He took full accountability for the decision. As the placard on his desk read, "The buck stops here." He never shirked the responsibility for his actions, despite the repercussions. In his farewell address to the American people in January 1953, Truman referred to this concept very specifically, asserting that,

"The president – whoever he is – has to decide. He can't pass the buck to anybody. No one else can do the deciding for him. That's his job."[58]

Brave

Being brave is core to outstanding leadership. Great leaders have a courageous mindset. They believe in themselves without limits. Importantly, brave leaders are not afraid to be vulnerable. They are prepared to break the rules for the better of everyone, step outside their comfort zone, ask the tough questions, have the hard conversations, and make the hard decisions.

As I've already stated, vulnerability is seen by many as a sign of weakness when, in fact, it is a sign of courage. Brave leaders are prepared to admit their mistakes. They dare to say, "Sorry, I messed up," or "I made a mistake." It encourages others to do the same, ensuring fewer mistakes are swept under the carpet.

Brave leaders also admit when they are struggling. For example, there may be times when you are not at the top of your game due to your health or matters in your personal life. It is okay to let other people (including your team) know about it. Vulnerability is not about sharing an exhaustive narrative about the disagreement you and your partner are currently having. No one needs a blow-by-blow account of the last heated conversation you had. It is enough to say that an issue at home is causing you some angst, but you are working toward a compromise with your partner.

Microsoft CEO Satya Nadella[59] is an excellent example of a vulnerable leader. In 2021, amid the COVID-19 pandemic, Nadella shared his feelings in a memo to employees:

"Much is unknown, and I know how unsettling and uncertain this feels. Like many of you, there have been times over the past weeks where it has felt overwhelming and all-encompassing for me. I worry about the health and safety of my family, my co-workers, and friends. My wife and I worry for her aging parents, who are far away from us in India. I see the struggle in our local community, and around the world, the empty streets and restaurants, and I wonder when our social fabric will be restored."[60]

He didn't just say, "I know how you must be feeling." He shared his fears and concerns to demonstrate his understanding.

Another example is the former CEO of Starbucks, Howard Schultz.[61] In 2008, at the height of the global financial crisis, he returned to the CEO role at the global coffee chain. Over 600 Starbucks stores had closed, resulting in mass layoffs. Approximately 12,000 employees lost their jobs. In his first week back, Howard stood before his entire company to apologize, and cried.

He later equated his moment of vulnerability with transparency, a key attribute in business leaders. In an interview with Oprah Winfrey, he said, "I think the currency of leadership is transparency. You've got to be truthful. I don't think you should be vulnerable every day, but there are moments where you've got to share your soul and conscience with people and show them who you are, and not be afraid of it."[62]

Here are some suggestions to become more vulnerable in your role as a leader and, in doing so, demonstrate bravery.

Intelligent disobedience

Great leaders are brave enough to challenge the status quo and are also prepared to break the rules for the benefit of others. They do not break them for personal gain but for the greater good. Of course, there are some rules you should not break, especially those related to health, safety, or security. However, leaders will break rules when they result in better outcomes for employees, consumers, customers, and the organization.

They will also break the rules when they know that following them will endanger their team or the organization. It is what could be termed *intelligent disobedience*. People usually use this term in relation to a service animal that disobeys its owner's instructions, knowing that following them could be harmful. It also has a place in transport, medicine, engineering, and business. In business, it is the courage to question decisions or instructions and suggest an alternative action to protect the team and/or the business.

In his book *Intelligent Disobedience: The Difference between Good and Great Leaders*, Bob McGannon explains how his perspective on leadership changed in a hotel lobby in San Jose, California.[63] He was waiting for an elevator along with a man with a seeing-eye dog. The elevator car reached the lobby but did not land correctly. It had stopped about eight inches below floor level, presenting a potential hazard to someone entering the elevator. What had been a calm and docile dog suddenly leaped into action and placed itself at a ninety-degree angle in front of its owner. It created a barrier between its owner and the danger. Bob explained what had happened to the dog's owner, and the owner informed Bob that the action was called intelligent disobedience. The owner had indicated what he wanted the dog to do, but the dog disobeyed and protected its owner from harm.

In the same way, leaders must possess the courage to oppose management decisions and directions if that opposition will help protect the organization from harm. Leaders must also encourage their team to practice intelligent disobedience. They do it by creating an environment of psychological safety. Leaders must ensure that everyone knows they can seek support from others and are not on their own. Leaders must enable everyone to have the courage to speak up or act differently.

Developing intelligent disobedience is a process. When intelligent disobedience has resulted in the right outcome, you should recognize and celebrate it. If it did not, adaptation is needed, and you must learn from the mistake. It is essential to recognize the intent while making improvements. We discuss recognition in more detail in "Empowering."

In August 1997, Korean Air flight 801 from Seoul was on descent into Guam. There was reduced visibility due to bad weather, which forced an instrument landing. The captain, Yong Park, had already indicated that he was fatigued. He began approaching a runway that was not in service, mistaking an irrelevant electronic device signal on the ground for the instrument landing system (ILS). The first officer and flight engineer pointed out that the airport was not visible, the beacon signal was incorrect, and the descent was too steep. Park continued and crashed into Bijia Peak, killing 229 of the 254 people on board.

The investigation found many issues, but what proved fatal was that the first officer and flight engineer did not challenge the captain's decision even though they knew he was wrong. Had they practiced intelligent disobedience, protested vehemently, and taken over the controls, the outcome would have been very different. Also, Korean culture highly values respect and hierarchy. It prevented the officer and engineer from disobeying what they knew would be a fatal decision. In the same way, you must work to build a culture in which everyone feels safe to challenge and take alternative action when they know that a decision or course of action will be detrimental to the organization.

Moving out of your comfort zone

Leaders with a brave mindset know that if they stay in their **comfort zone**, nothing will change. The comfort zone is where you feel calm and safe, but not much is happening. There is not much movement or learning. When you are in this zone, there is no growth. It is okay to be in this zone sometimes, but, if you stay too long, the comfort zone shrinks as you become more and more fearful as more things don't feel safe.

Figure 24: Comfort zone to terror zone

Where you need to be for learning, development, and growth is in the **stretch zone**.

The best place to sit is *on the edge* between the comfort zone and the stretch zone. Expansion happens when you dance on the edge of the comfort zone so you can move to and from the stretch zone. There is a tingly mixture of fear, excitement, trepidation, and anticipation. As you move between the zones, your courage and bravery grow.

It is where you push yourself to improve. You leave your comfort zone and have the courage to try new things. You are daring and brave in this zone. Yes, there is stress in this zone, but this is good stress. Not all stress is bad. Good stress is a result of being vulnerable and exposed. You probably feel edgy and excited in this zone, and the adrenaline is pumping.

The more time you spend in the stretch zone, the bigger your comfort zone grows. You grow more confident and independent. You increase your passion and perseverance, which equals grit. You become more and more courageous. You become more adaptable to change, which increases your resilience. It is where the magic happens!

Where you do not want to be is in the **terror zone**. It is the danger zone. It is where the bad stress happens. It is where you will be overwhelmed and burnt out. At the earliest opportunity, you will return to your comfort zone, which will start shrinking again. In this zone, there is panic and extreme anxiety.

You will feel vulnerable and exposed when you step outside your comfort zone, but this is not a reason not to step outside. You will deny yourself the courage to lead, and your comfort zone will shrink. When you dance on the edge, you become more courageous and grow.

What you step outside of your comfort zone for depends on what type of leadership style you seek – and what kind of leader you wish to be. You could try improving your communication and listening skills, collaborating, leading working groups, public speaking, and deepening your emotional intelligence. Keep stepping into the stretch zone and practicing. You will become stronger and more confident; building confidence is critical to becoming a brave leader.

Staying inside your comfort zone is like a ship staying in a harbor. That is not what the ship was built for. Like a ship intended to sail the oceans, you must push your boundaries and unlock your leadership capabilities.

What's the worst that can happen?

The brave leader asks, "What's the worst that can happen?" When you pause to ask this question, you put a space between you and your fear. The worst thing is often not that bad; that realization can spur you to act. If the worst thing that can happen is really bad, then perhaps this is an action you do not want to take.

However, when you fixate on the worst possible outcome and treat it as likely to happen, even when it is not, this is called catastrophizing. It means you have jumped to the worst possible conclusion, often with no supporting facts or reasons. If you are going for an interview, you catastrophize when you tell yourself you will fail if you do not get the job. When you want to tell the boss their decision may not be the best, you catastrophize when you tell yourself that you will lose your job and never be able to work in that industry again. Your imagination can wreak havoc with your mental health.

So, you need to be specific. Clearly define what you are fearing. How likely is it to happen? What is the possible damage? When you make it clear, you remove the vague threats and risks. Your imagination may also tell you that you cannot undertake a particular task. Again, be specific. What action can you take? What options do you have?

You can also put things into perspective. How much would people care if you were to deliver a speech that did not go so well? How invested are people in your life and your shortcomings? Most people can bounce forward after a setback, such as losing a job, making a mistake, or failing to seize an opportunity. When you put things into perspective, you see them more objectively.

Having hard conversations

Brave leaders are not afraid to have the hard conversations. They do not avoid them.

When you label a conversation as "difficult" in advance, you see the situation through a particular frame that will make you feel uneasy, nervous, or anxious. Reframe the conversation as a positive one. Rather than thinking you are giving someone negative feedback on their performance, see it as a conversation that will help them grow and develop. Offer an alternative solution rather than saying "no" to an employee.

The hardest conversation should not be the first. If an employee is not performing and you have decided that letting them go will be the best for them, the team, and the organization, you should have had many conversations before that final one. There should be no surprises. There must be a mutual understanding of why the conversation is taking place. If this is a termination conversation, make sure you have engaged HR for advice.

You must facilitate hard conversations with empathy, which we've discussed at length. You must be able to actively listen and ensure mutual understanding. Having said that, ensure that data and facts, not hearsay, support these conversations. Make sure they happen promptly. Don't procrastinate and drag your feet. The situation could deteriorate and make the conversation harder than needed if held earlier.

If you do not have a hard conversation with a team member regarding their behavior or performance, it can devastate the rest of the team. They will be aware of the person's under-performance or conflictive behavior. They will suffer due to the behavior itself and potentially being forced to pick up the slack. If you do not have the conversation, you're essentially saying you do not care and that the team should tolerate the situation.

When you have the conversation, you are saying that neither you nor the team should accept the situation, and you will take action to rectify it. When the team knows you will have these conversations when necessary, they know you have their back. They will trust you.

Making hard decisions

I read an article in the *Australian Financial Review* by Amantha Imber (organizational psychologist) about decision-making.[64] She raised the question of whether decisions are hard or just unpleasant. I think she is on to something.

Take some examples of what we consider hard decisions: firing an underperforming employee, having to let employees go due to financial constraints, reporting sexual misconduct of a superior in the workplace, or pulling a project that is no longer a priority. When you look at these decisions, you already know the correct answer. The issue is not that the decision is hard but unpleasant.

If you have to fire an underperforming employee and have been performance managing regularly, there should be no surprise to the employee. It is never pleasant to fire someone, but not doing so adversely impacts the team. As stated in the previous section, they see no action being taken about an under-performer while they are potentially carrying that person's workload.

Letting employees go due to financial constraints is also unpleasant. If the organization is going through tough times financially, and the only option available is to reduce the headcount, then it is not a hard one – it's unpleasant. You should decide promptly to ensure the rest of the workforce does not feel threatened.

If you notice sexual misconduct by a person in a more senior position, it should not be hard to report it, but may be unpleasant to do so. If you know that no one will listen to you and no one will investigate the case, I suggest looking for a new job. That is a toxic workplace, and you deserve better than that. It may be unpleasant, but it becomes easy when considering the implications of not reporting the conduct. You will know you are guilty of duplicity and must live with that. The misconduct you've witnessed will repeat if you don't stop it. You have a duty of care to your employees to provide a mentally and physically safe environment.

It is unpleasant to pull a project that is popular to work on. The fact that it is no longer a priority, for whatever reason, should not make it a hard decision. You will waste time and money that could be better allocated to projects driving organizational success. The hard thing for you as a leader is to embrace the discomfort of making the decision, knowing you are doing the right thing.

In Amantha Imber's words, "By recognizing a decision's true nature and taking the bull by the horns, you can optimize your decision-making process, keep stress at bay, and boost your chances of success. So, the next time you're at a crossroads, remember to ask yourself whether you're dealing with a genuine brain-teaser or just an irksome choice, and act accordingly."

You may need to make decisions fast depending on the context in which you find yourself. However, whenever possible, you should do some detective work to ensure you make the right decision:

- Investigate the issue.
- Break down complex problems to prioritize your investigations.
- Gather information.
- Search records.
- Collect evidence.
- Observe activities.
- Liaise with other functional areas.
- Ask questions. Seek feedback. Ask more questions.

- Communicate. Listen, be empathetic, and tune into people's reactions.
- Employ deductive reasoning and analysis to make informed decisions.
- Testify regarding the evidence and findings to support your decision.

Managing successful change

Research has revealed that managing successful change is a skill most leaders need to develop.[65] Plenty of information is available across the internet on managing successful change. Just do a Google search of those words – "how to manage successful change" – and I suspect you will get millions of results. I want to bolster the guidance and highlight five mistakes I see leaders making that adversely impact their chances of achieving successful change. Some of these have been explored elsewhere in this book in different contexts, so I'll keep them fairly brief.

Starting from the wrong place

When discussing a forthcoming change, many leaders start to talk about what the organization will do and how it will do it. The need for a change often originates in the "corner office," and leaders neglect to explain the "why" behind it. They focus on "what" and "how" it needs to change. They make the blind assumption that everyone will know the "why." Isn't it obvious? No, not necessarily. Starting with why creates a sense of urgency, as there is recognition regarding what will happen if the organization does not change. If the organization does nothing, ultimately nobody will have a job.

Communicating rather than having a conversation

Leaders managing successful change need to recognize the difference between having conversations with stakeholders and communicating with stakeholders. I often hear leaders say that they have communicated – just last week via email, perhaps. My response is that their action was a broadcast and undeniably one-way. If leaders think about having a conversation rather than delivering communication, the one-way mode is eradicated. More on this in the next section of the book.

Thinking you must have all the answers

So many leaders believe they must have all the answers because they are in a leadership position. Yet, no one ever said that when you become a leader, you also become the fountain of all knowledge! When managing successful change, openness, honesty, and transparency are key. You must say, "I don't know the answer, but let me go and find out." The worst thing you can do is make up an answer to a question because it is certain to come back and bite you when proven incorrect.

Not soliciting feedback

When managing successful change, leaders must solicit feedback from stakeholders at all organizational levels and positions. This critical feedback lets leaders know whether communication and engagement work as intended, if the direction is correct, and what problems they might anticipate, among other things. Soliciting feedback must be done regularly and act as a checkpoint to determine if everything is on track.

Leaders may encounter resistance to change when seeking feedback, but that is not necessarily bad. Resistance to change can be a good thing. If people resist change, it means they have started their change journey. They are no longer in denial that a change is happening but have recognized that they will need to change and adopt a new way of working. So, anticipate the resistance that your change may encounter and embrace it. It's a good thing! Having said that, if you encounter substantial resistance to a change, it might indicate the change is unwise, and you should stop it in its tracks to prevent a disastrous failure.

A lack of engagement

The final of the five mistakes is not engaging with stakeholders enough. This often happens as it is time-consuming and there are conflicting priorities. However, a lack of engagement could signal the demise of the change. Engagement, in whatever form, should enable stakeholders to seek out more information, raise concerns, ask questions, participate in user-experience sessions, engage in scenario testing, and get closer to the change that is taking place. When stakeholders can get involved in the change, they have skin in the game to make the change a success. When you create a sense of engagement, it will result in ownership of the change.

Real-world example: Malala Yousafzai

Malala Yousafzai[66] is a Pakistani woman who is the epitome of a brave leader, as she was prepared to break the rules. She was born on July 12, 1997, in Mingora, Pakistan. Her father was a teacher and ran a girls' school in the village. Malala loved school. Unfortunately, when the Taliban took control of the village in 2008, Malala was told she could no longer go to school. The Taliban also banned many things like television and playing music. Those who defied their orders suffered harsh punishments.

Malala was eleven years old.

She spoke out publicly against the prohibition on girls' education. Then, in 2012, a masked man boarded her school bus and asked, "Who is Malala?" He shot her in the left side of her head. The Taliban took full responsibility for the attempt on her life. Mullah Fazlullah, Taliban leader, had lifted the ban on girls attending school until their exams were held on a particular date, but they had to wear burqas.

Malala was fifteen years old.

She survived the attack and was flown from Peshawar to the UK, for surgery. The event sparked an international outpouring of support. In response, the Taliban further denounced her and threatened a second assassination attempt.

After months of surgery and rehabilitation, she was discharged from the hospital on January 3, 2013, and continued her rehabilitation at the family's temporary home in the West Midlands. On February 2, she underwent a five-hour operation to reconstruct her skull and restore her hearing.

For the first time since being shot, she made a public appearance on July 12, 2013, addressing a crowd of 500 at the United Nations in New York City. The UN dubbed the event "Malala Day." She had an audience with Queen Elizabeth II in Buckingham Palace, and, in September, she spoke at Harvard University. In October, she met with then US President Barack Obama. In December, she addressed the Oxford Union.

In 2013, she and her father founded the Malala Fund to champion every girl's right to twelve years of free, safe, quality education.

Malala was sixteen years old.

On October 10, 2014, she received the Nobel Peace Prize, making her the youngest Nobel Peace laureate.

Malala was seventeen years old.

Following the completion of her education in the UK, she returned to Pakistan and continues her activism. With nearly 120 million girls out of school today, she fights to break down the barriers that hold girls back. Her bravery, accompanied by humility, is summed up in this statement:

"I tell my story not because it is unique but because it is not. It is the story of many girls."[67]

Listening

Despite this chapter being called "Listening," I will also explore communicating, as you must communicate effectively to listen actively.

Both communicating and listening require a mindset. The communicating mindset drives you to think and be intentional about the purpose of your communication, analyze your different audiences, and be empathetic about their needs. The listening mindset allows you to listen, empathize, and understand the other person's feelings. It enables you to be present, attentive, and non-judgmental.

In October 1990, I worked for the UK Post Office and undertook the Dale Carnegie Management Seminar. I know the date as I still have my completion certificate!

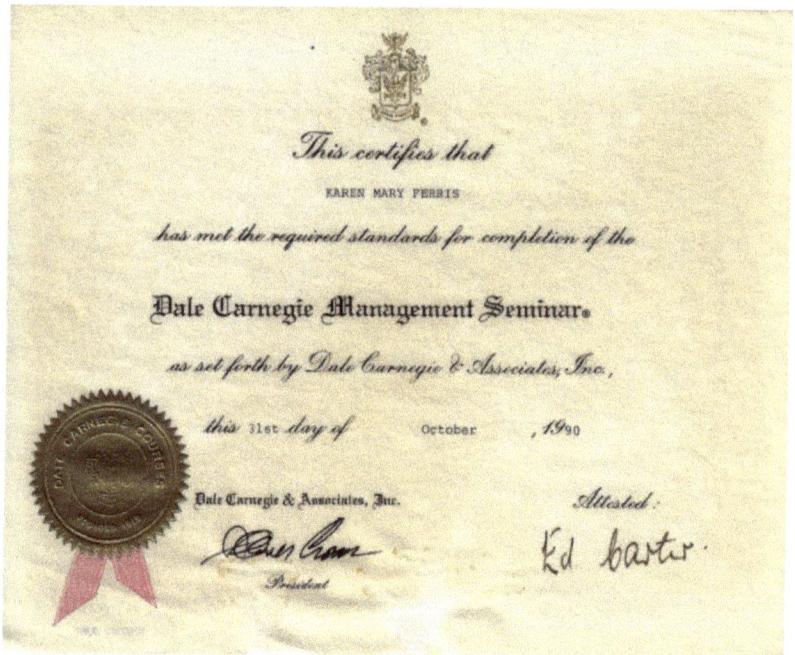

Figure 25: Dale Carnegie Management Seminar completion certificate

The seminar presented me with the 1987 edition of Dale Carnegie & Associates' book *Managing Through People*.[68] At the time of writing, that was thirty-six years ago. One of the critical elements of the seminar and the book was effective communication and listening. Dale Carnegie[69] first wrote about being a good communicator and listener in his 1936 book *How to Win Friends and Influence People*. That was nearly eight decades ago, and it has sold tens of millions of copies since then.

Authors have written much more about effective communication and active listening over the years, but people are not reading these works. It is a crying shame when you consider the fact that communication and listening are two of the most critical skills you need as a leader.

Since authors have written extensively on this matter, I do not intend to replicate their work here. I want to explore with you the impact of ineffective communication and poor listening, together with some of the critical mistakes I observe and how you can avoid them.

Ineffective communication can have devastating effects. Lack of communication or confusing messages can lead to misunderstanding, conflict, friction, confusion, frustration, and a disengaged workforce. Poor communication will result in an erosion of trust between you and your employees. Effective communication promotes a transparent culture, whereas poor communication promotes uncertainty and doubt.

The impact of not listening manifests itself in many ways. You cannot empathize if you do not listen. You can only provide direction if you listen. You can only offer support if you listen. You can only coach or mentor if you listen. You can only communicate effectively if you listen, as you know your message has been received as intended.

You should be able to build good communication skills and effective listening, but that is where leaders make their biggest mistakes. They still fail to communicate and listen proficiently despite all the guidance available. As I work with organizations, I regularly observe the inadequacy of these two skills. This is why I continue to run customized communication and active listening workshops for employees at all levels of the organization, including those designated as leaders. Unless you get this right, all your leadership development will be like building a house on shifting sand. In other words, you will be wasting both your time and your money.

I think people assume their communication and listening skills must be okay because they "communicate" and "listen" all the time. This is not the case. Just because you can speak does not mean you are communicating. Just because you can hear does not mean you are listening. It is time to relearn these skills.

Relearning the skill of communication

To this day, I still hear people saying, "We did communicate with them. We sent them an email." My response? "That is not communication. That is a broadcast." It is a one-way announcement. It does not always evoke a response. In this section, I share some key insights and tips to relearn the skill of communication.

Communication < conversation

If you stopped to think about communication as a conversation, the chances of you getting it right would increase. You should not direct communication *at* your audience, but instead engage in it *with* them.

I created an infographic to isolate the ten critical differences between communication and conversation.

COMMUNICATION	CONVERSATION
Monologue	Dialogue
May not solicit a response	Solicits a response
Distributes information	Creates understanding
Implies one party has more weight than the other	All parties have equal importance
May not involve listening	Involves listening
Single event to move towards an outcome	Continuous engagement to achieve an outcome
Transmits facts	Transforms, reshapes
Know audience wants and needs	Determine audience wants and needs
Passive consumers	Active consumers
Exclusive	Inclusive

Figure 26: Communication versus conversation

© 2024 Karen Ferris

When you communicate like you are having a conversation, you transmit a message and check that the message was received as intended. Let's explore the differences between communication and having a conversation.

Monologue versus dialogue

A monologue is typically a person's speech, and interaction is absent. It is when someone is talking *at* you. In contrast, a dialogue is when someone talks with you. It is a conversation between two or more people. The upside of dialogue is that you must listen. If you are not listening, you are not leading people or change in your organization. It never ceases to amaze me how tirelessly organizations work to hire smart people. Then, they wonder why those employees get frustrated when they are not involved in a conversation about change. Smart people want to be a part of the conversation — not be talked at. They want to be involved.

Leadership is about building relationships, and that comes about through understanding others — their perspectives, views, ideas, values, and aspirations. You can only accomplish that through having a conversation and dialogue. To quote *Dialogue* author William Isaacs, "Dialogue, as I define it, is a conversation with a center, not sides. It is a way of taking the energy of our differences and channeling it toward something that has never been created before. It lifts us out of polarization and into a greater common sense, and is thereby a means for accessing the intelligence and coordinated power of groups of people."[70]

May not solicit a response versus solicits a response

Much communication happens in one way, neither soliciting nor receiving a response. There are two distinct outcomes.

When communication is a broadcast, an announcement, or a notification, it is not asking for employee feedback. It does not encourage employees to ask questions or seek further clarification. People should accept this blanket statement at its face value. For employees, that is like being in a dictatorship. My way or the highway. Welcome to the Great Resignation.

When communication asks for a response and encourages employees to provide feedback, it often does not happen. The nature of the communication infers it is a done deal, so employees feel there is little point in sharing their thoughts. History may also have shown that feedback is requested but not listened to, which deters employees from responding. Communication aims to convey a message. A conversation seeks to have a discussion.

A conversation, therefore, explicitly solicits feedback. Only by requesting a response do you find out what employees are thinking. If you do not hear what they are thinking and act accordingly, you are just doing change *to* people rather than *with* them, and that will result in change failure. You must provide various channels for employees to respond. The most important thing is to indicate that you have received the response, listened, and will take action. Failure to do so results in future requests for feedback not being met.

Distributes information versus creates understanding

Communication is the conveyance of a formed idea. It distributes information via a well-curated message to a defined set of recipients. Conversation ensures understanding.

If you just communicate, you have no idea whether your message was received as intended. Communication doesn't check that the message's language, form, or tone resonated with the audience and was understood.

A conversation always ensures an understanding as it cannot occur unless both parties speak in a language and form understood by the other. A conversation also allows a check to ensure the message is understood as intended. We can all interpret what we have heard in different ways. Two people can hear the same words and take away different ideas.

A conversation can verify what people have heard, not just what has been dispatched. If the message is not understood as intended, it can be adjusted and revised accordingly. It is dangerous if messages about change are interpreted in different ways by different people. It leads to uncertainty, anxiety, and stress. What one person heard differed from what another heard, which means no one is clear about the reality.

Implies one party has more weight versus all parties have equal importance

When communication is one-sided and unidirectional, it implies that the party delivering the message is more important than the recipients. When you do not solicit a response, it says that someone who knows better than everyone else has made the decisions and does not need any input, thoughts, or ideas.

When you have a conversation, all parties are of equal importance. You hear every voice, and thoughts and ideas are exchanged. It is often the employees who are closer to the customer, and closer to the action and operational aspects of the business, who know whether an idea is a good one or not. What might seem like a good idea from the boardroom may seem like a bad one on the factory floor. If you want to make a change, don't do it to people – do it with them or they will eventually go elsewhere.

May not involve listening versus involves listening

Communication does not have to involve listening, whereas conversation *must* include listening. You can only have a bidirectional discussion by listening to the other participants. You need to listen and understand what others say to respond appropriately.

Active listening means listening attentively to the person speaking and understanding what they are saying. To do this, you seek clarity, reflect on what you have heard, and respond accordingly. Perhaps you're wondering, "How do I do this in large groups? How do I actively listen to the entire workforce?" You use other leaders, teams, and agents of change. These are the people who should be listening to the feedback from employees and relaying it to you. These are the people paying attention, indicating that they are listening, avoiding distraction, deferring judgment, clarifying what they have heard, and responding appropriately.

Single event to move toward an outcome versus continuous engagement

Communication is a one-off event intended to move recipients toward an outcome. It is a one-off event designed to coax, coerce, and convince recipients to move into a particular position. I see this in organizations where the initiator of a change is so convinced of its legitimacy and need that they assume everyone else will see it similarly. Rarely is this the case.

A conversation is a series of continuous engagements to achieve an outcome. This conversation starts with why. Why is a change needed? So often, you begin with what will change and how it will change, and forget that you must start with why. For example, you issue a communication that says the organization will undertake a digital transformation (what), starting with artificial intelligence and machine learning (how). The only question employees want and need answering is why.

When there is a consensus on the "why," which could be to remain competitive and stay in business, everyone understands the outcome needed. Continuous engagement allows everyone to achieve the same outcome with a shared purpose and direction. It enables early identification of the need to change direction and take action.

Transmits facts versus transforms and reshapes

Historian and author Theodore Zeldin has stated, "Conversation is a meeting of minds with different memories and habits. When minds meet, they don't just exchange facts; they transform them, reshape them, draw different implications from them, and engage in new trains of thought. Conversation doesn't just reshuffle the cards: it creates new cards."[71]

Communication transmits facts, whereas conversation can transform and reshape ideas. Communication is transactional – it passes on factual information and does not allow for any kind of emotional response. Conversation, on the other hand, engages on an emotional level and enables transformation to happen.

Leaders who understand this establish a connection with their audience. They know that without connection, there can be no emotional response. They know their audience and what makes them tick. They can have a conversation that resonates with their audience and elicits ideas, feelings, and concerns. The elicitation and subsequent exchange can transform good ideas into great ideas and reshape the mundane into the extraordinary.

Know audience wants and needs versus determine audience wants and needs

When you communicate, you assume you know the wants and needs of the audience. The message has been well-honed and delivered in a careful and considered manner.

With conversations, there are no assumptions. You actively determine what the audience wants and needs. No assumptions are made, allowing you to adjust your engagement approach as necessary.

Passive consumers versus active consumers

When you communicate, the consumers of your words are passive. They are less likely to take any action, simply letting your words flow over them. There is no emotional connection or response. A passive audience can lead some to believe that their silence indicates agreement, but it is quite the opposite in most situations. They are silent because you present them with a decision already made and so they believe they cannot influence the decision or the outcome. The silent audience is the most dangerous, as they could be withholding critical feedback.

When you have a conversation, your consumers are active. They believe their opinions will be heard and valued, so they have some skin in the game. They are connected, engaged, and invested in the best outcome for themselves, the team, and the organization. They will share their thoughts, ideas, emotions, feelings, fears, and concerns. The conversation is a continuous engagement to uncover everything that will enable a change to be successful and all the things that will work against it. Change has a much greater chance of success when this conversation takes place.

Exclusive versus inclusive

Communication is exclusive, while conversation is inclusive. Communication is unidirectional and excludes the audience from being actively involved, providing feedback, and sharing ideas. When employees do not feel included, they do not feel valued. They do not have a sense of purpose or belonging.

Employees feel included when the organization embraces new ideas, perspectives, and views. Employees feel included when they are part of a conversation. They are more likely to share their ideas and opinions as they know they have a voice. They are connected and committed to the organization's well-being through a sense of belonging. They feel valued and appreciated.

Too many people hide behind the statement "People resist change." When a change goes awry, this statement is an excuse not to connect and explain. A conversation takes longer than communication. "If we assume people will resist the change whatever we do, then let's just communicate it. We will save time." I don't believe people resist change when it's done correctly. If you exclude people from change, they will resist it. When you include people in change, they will support it.

Utilize different channels

You must be authentic and utilize the various communication channels and mediums. You must not hide behind email and company bulletins. You must be accessible for people to ask questions, seek clarification, and raise concerns. You must know your audience and hone your communication to meet their needs or concerns. You must determine how often you will communicate, the message you will send, who will send it, and the desired outcome with each audience.

When considering the channels for communicating a change, ensure they are the ones that convey the message behind the change. If you put your communication in the old company bulletin that everyone finds boring and just deletes, you infer your change is boring. Find more exciting, dynamic, and different ways to communicate. Think about using video, gamification, infographics, animations, virtual digital signage or noticeboards, virtual reality communications, and storytelling.

One approach, which I have used successfully to communicate change, is to create a postcard from the future, which can be distributed physically or electronically. It contains a vibrant picture from the near future that shows what is possible. In essence, it is a picture of the vision for the change.

Put yourself in the future looking back, not in the present looking forward. The picture should excite and motivate people to find out more. Do this in a workshop format to solicit many ideas. The postcard should tell a compelling message and be somewhat futuristic. It should also be practical enough that it can be seen as achievable. As an example, I created this for a global organization that was struggling with collaboration. Silos had emerged. Divisions were operating independently resulting in inconsistent processes and duplication of effort. Everyone was aware of the issue and wanted change. The postcard introduced the future and the project to get there. It contained links to get further information.

Figure 27: Postcard from the future

Don't worry about over-communication

Refrain from letting anyone tell you that you can over-communicate. You cannot. If your message is clear, concise, consistent, and targeted, you can repeat it. There is a rule of seven based on a marketing principle that customers need to hear your message at least seven times before they will act. It doesn't mean you must stick to that exact number, but it demonstrates that repetition is essential.

If you announce a change, employees may be preoccupied or distracted, and their minds clouded with emotional reactions. They may only partially absorb the message when they first hear it. Each time you repeat it, they get another opportunity to learn about the change.

Research has found that leaders are ten times as likely to be criticized for under-communicating than for over-communicating. Leaders who under-communicate are seen as less qualified for a leadership role as they are viewed as less empathetic. When there is a lack of congruence between perceived and preferred communication, employees judge their leaders as lacking empathy and, in turn, leadership ability.[72]

I worked with a global organization undertaking a major change. The program appeared to be tracking well, but the feedback from the employees raised concern...

"I think I heard something is happening, but I am not sure what it is."

"I know there is change taking place, but I have no idea what it means to me."

"Remind me again which change you are talking about."

"I am concerned because I don't know enough."

All this feedback indicated a lack of communication. Communication had taken place, but, unfortunately, it was assumed that one email would be enough. As George Bernard Shaw said, "The single biggest problem in communication is the illusion that it has taken place."[73]

The lack of communication was causing fear, uncertainty, and stress. I assisted the transformation team in first understanding why communication was critical to the program's success and, secondly, how to communicate effectively, including frequency The message must be repeated many times and in many ways. You must remember that you have many audiences and how they receive the message depends on where they stand. The program was successful in part because of a collective and consistent understanding of the reason for the change, what was changing, and how. Everyone understood what it meant for them.

Use the appropriate questions

When you are having a conversation, you should be asking questions. You can use questions to confirm that your message was received as intended. You can also use questions to learn more about your audience and their needs, concerns, expectations, and opinions. It helps to tailor your messages, and it also makes employees feel valued.

Consider the outcomes you wish to achieve from your conversation and use the appropriate questions. These could include:

- **Open questions:** Ask these to encourage the other person to elaborate or explain. These questions can uncover things you may not have thought to ask about. Example: "How did you feel about that last meeting?"
- **Closed questions:** Ask these for short, specific answers such as "Yes" or "No." Use these for fact-finding or guiding

a conversation in a particular way to obtain specific information from which you can then formulate an open question. Example: "Was that last meeting all right?"

- **Confirmation questions:** Ask these to ensure the other person understands your message. Example: "What were you feeling when that meeting ended?"
- **Playback questions:** Ask these to summarize the conversation and clarify your understanding of the other person's needs. Example: "I would like to summarize what you have told me. You found the meeting too long and unstructured?"

Of course, these questions are only valuable if you are listening.

Harness storytelling and the power of pictures

Storytelling is a highly effective communication method. Stories are illustrative, easily memorable, and allow the communicator to create stronger emotional bonds with the recipients. When you hear stories, you are more engaged than you would be by just hearing about data and facts.

When you read or listen to data alone, the language part of the brain works to understand it. When you read or hear a story, not only does the language part of the brain start to work, but other parts of the brain start working too. It is far easier to remember stories than data or facts.

One of the best ways to tell stories, or enhance them, is through pictures. It is not a cliché when people say, "A picture paints a thousand words." It is true. For example, which of these is easier to understand?

A circle is a simple, closed shape. It is the set of all points in a plane that are at a given distance from a given point, the center; equivalently, it is the curve traced out by a point that moves in a plane so that its distance from a given point is constant. (Wikipedia)

OR

Figure 28: Circle – words vs. picture

If you can use images and graphics to enhance your message, do so.

The key is to know your audience. In some instances, relying on text or imagery alone to convey your message is not the best approach. In fact, it can lead to disaster.

Let me share a cautionary tale. Anyone who has assembled Ikea[74] furniture knows the instruction manual is wordless – just illustrations. It enables Ikea to have customers worldwide without printing assembly instructions in many different languages. The drawback is that not everyone is good at translating the illustrations, so important instructions and warnings may get overlooked. In recent years, the tipping over of Ikea dressers has tragically killed several children.[75]

Ikea has claimed that it warns buyers to anchor such items to a wall to prevent them from tipping over, but image-only instructions are insufficient for such important warnings. Ikea had to create a series of TV advertisements about anchoring large furniture items. It was an expensive exercise on top of multimillion-dollar settlements for the families affected by Ikea's major oversight.

The lesson is to know your audience and ensure that important messages are conveyed in the clearest, most consistent way possible so that they are received and understood.

Relearning the skill of listening

I have touched on active listening, as it is hard to talk about communication without referencing listening. Let's look at it in more depth.

Active listening enables you to obtain information, understand, and learn. When you practice active listening, you consciously strive to hear the words spoken and, more importantly, understand the complete message communicated.

The Dale Carnegie & Associates' book *Managing Through People*, which I mentioned earlier, includes a quiz that I thought I would use to help you understand if you are an active listener and determine areas for improvement.

Do you stop talking while someone is trying to tell you something?

You cannot listen if you are talking. Period.

Listen rather than think about what you want to say. Give the other person your full and undivided attention. Use non-verbal feedback such as nodding, facial expressions, and the right body language to reassure the person you are listening to. Maintain eye contact, turn your head and torso to face the person speaking, and lean forward to show them you are interested and paying attention. Show you are listening by uncrossing your arms and legs. Put your feet flat on the floor, and use open palms to invite the other person to speak.

Do you concentrate on what is said and make eye contact?

When you are an active listener, you avoid all distractions. You cannot allow yourself to be distracted by what is going on around you. This includes noise from incoming messages, phone calls, and emails. If you check messages when someone is talking to you, you are telling that person they are not a priority and you are not interested in what they say.

You must give the speaker your undivided attention and acknowledge that you are listening by making eye contact, whereby you and another person look into each other's eyes *at the same time*. You can tell when someone is looking elsewhere, even if they don't move their head. You can observe the direction of their gaze, and, if they keep looking in the same direction for an extended period, it indicates they are not concentrating on you.

You do not have to stare at the other person like you are trying to hypnotize them! Hold your eye contact for four to five seconds at a time. Make eye contact before you speak. As a rule of thumb, you should maintain eye contact fifty to seventy per cent of the time during your conversation.

Making eye contact helps you to remember what the other person said. It also creates a bond with the other person. It is an important display of honesty and authenticity, building trust and respect. It improves understanding between people by helping you to focus and read the non-verbal clues about how the other person is feeling, such as their facial expressions.

Do you listen to the whole story without interrupting?

As Stephen Covey said in his book *The 7 Habits of Highly Successful People*[76], most people do not listen with the intent to understand; they listen with the intent to reply.

Test this out. Next time you are in a conversation, note how long the other person speaks before your mind is immediately seeking a way to reply. When you are formulating a reply, it is extremely difficult to listen to what the other person is saying.

Interrupting stops the other person from speaking. You cut them off. It is human nature to want to connect and help another person, but interrupting will negatively impact the connection. You have shifted the focus of the conversation to you. And it's rude.

It also means you do not get the entire story. It can be dangerous. In 1984, Howard Beckman and Richard M. Frankel[77] conducted a study that revealed how long a doctor would let a patient talk without interrupting them. The average time was just eighteen seconds. They concluded that this behavior could cause doctors to lose valuable information vital to arriving at a correct diagnosis for their patients. Now, while you may not be diagnosing a medical condition, you could be providing advice or guidance that will be ill-informed because you have not listened to the entire story.

You may interrupt to ask a question, provide a solution to a problem, or show that you understand, but, just like being distracted, it tells the other person that you don't care what they have to say and want to end the conversation. It tells the other person that your voice is more important and you don't have time to listen to them.

You must learn to listen to the full story before speaking. You must let the other person finish speaking before you ask your question, offer a solution, or provide your opinion. Avoiding interruption makes the conversation more meaningful and productive. It shows respect for the other person and encourages open dialogue. It will enhance your understanding of the other person's message and emotions, and build trust.

So, be aware of when you are interrupting. This self-awareness makes you aware of the situations where it is likely to happen. It also lets you acknowledge to the other person that you know what you just did and are working to improve. A simple "Sorry, I just interrupted you, please carry on," will suffice. In this way, you can get the conversation back on track.

Here are some tips to avoid interrupting:

- Wait until there is a natural break in the conversation.
- Stop formulating your responses and just listen.
- Make eye contact.
- Reflect on what the other person said, summarize it, and play it back to them. Then you can share your thoughts.
- Be non-judgmental. You are likely to interrupt when you are judgmental and disagree with what is said.
- Don't assume you know what the other person is going to say. Assuming you know nothing forces you to listen.
- Don't try to find a solution when you should be listening.
- If you are formulating questions instead of listening, you will be more likely to interrupt. So, hold off on the questions.
- Ask the other person if they have finished before you speak.

Do you refrain from injecting your ideas and opinions, and finishing the other person's sentences for them?

This is a very annoying habit that many people have. When someone is talking and pauses to find the right words or gather their thoughts, the other person feels the need to fill the silence and start talking. Let the silence sit there for a while. It is not a vacuum that you must fill.

When you finish a person's sentence for them, you have broken the flow of the conversation. You've made a terrible mistake in assuming you knew what they would say. In most cases, you probably get it wrong and have thrown the other person right off track. If you finish someone else's sentences, they will feel you are putting words in their mouth.

Your goal is to listen, so avoid jumping in with your ideas and opinions. Before you enter and during the conversation, remove your biases and be non-judgmental. While your ideas and opinions may be valid, while you are formulating them, you are not listening. While you are injecting them, you are not listening. Just like interrupting, when you recognize you are finishing other people's sentences, you can take action to avoid it.

Here are some ways to avoid finishing other people's sentences:

- Be patient if the person speaking is speaking slowly or is hesitant. Let them have time to tell you their story in its completeness. Relax.
- Ask others to tell you when you are finishing their sentences to increase your self-awareness.

- Watch the other person's mouth. You can normally tell when they have finished speaking, and, if you are unsure, ask them if they still have more to add. Do not make them feel that you are wrapping up the conversation by finishing their sentences.

- Be aware of the other person's reaction when you have finished their sentence. Do they appear irritated, annoyed, disappointed, frustrated, or hurt? When you realize your impact, it will help you change your behavior.

Do you give the impression that you are genuinely interested in what is said?

If you want someone to tell you their feelings or share their ideas, they must know you are genuinely interested.

There are many ways in which to do this:

- Face the person who is talking to you.
- Make eye contact.
- Open up and relax. Do not create a barrier by crossing your arms or ankles, or putting your hands in your pockets.
- Nod to signal you are engaged, interested, and understanding. Nodding encourages the other person to keep talking.
- As you are nodding, try simple utterances such as, "Ah-ha" or "Mmhmm" or "I see." It keeps the conversation moving.
- Use facial expressions to reflect what is said. Smile, frown, and raise your eyebrows as is fitting.
- Lean in so they know you are listening.
- Empathize by using the same facial expressions.

- Ask questions without constantly interrupting. Ask permission to ask a question. It shows you are interested in what they say and want to know more.
- When the other person finishes speaking, reflect and use your own words to summarize what they have said so they know you were listening.

Real-world example: Titanic

The sinking of the Titanic[78] on April 14, 1912, resulted in the deaths of over 1,500 people. On the night of the sinking, wireless operators Jack Phillips and Harold Bride had received multiple warnings of icebergs in the waters ahead. They passed the message to the bridge, but listening failed. Captain Edward Smith did alter course slightly, but he did not slow the ship down, appearing to not fully understand the message or not take it seriously.

Phillips and Bride were also extremely busy sending and receiving passenger social messages, as well as dealing with incoming messages from other ships warning of ice fields. The first was from the *Mesaba*. Later, one came from the liner *Californian*, reporting that it had stopped and was surrounded by ice. Rather than listen to the *Californian* report, Phillips chastised the ship's officer for interrupting him when he was so busy with passenger messages.

Failure of the wireless operators and the captain to listen to the other ships' messages, understand them, and seek clarification resulted in the *Titanic*'s collision with an iceberg that sank the ship.

Empowering

Leaders with an empowering mindset provide their employees with the autonomy to make their own decisions and own their work. They provide the tools, resources, and support needed. This environment of empowerment increases employee engagement, creativity, innovation, and motivation. Research has shown it can also boost job satisfaction, organizational commitment, and task and contextual performance, while reducing employee strain and turnover intentions.[79]

The opposite leadership style of empowerment is command and control. This has its roots in the military, where strict hierarchies, top-down authority, and defined chains of command were thought essential to win on the battlefield.

As military leaders returned from war and into the workforce after World War II, the command and control leadership style made its way into factories where management believed that standardized and repeatable processes needed a top-down approach to ensure adherence. At this time, there was also the prevailing belief in many societies that there was value in authority, hierarchy, discipline, and clear delineation of roles and responsibilities. Therefore, command and control became an entrenched leadership style. The leader was set apart by their position and had sole decision-making authority, and teams followed orders as directed.

Command and control leadership has an impact. Employees have no autonomy or authority to make decisions. There is no room for creativity, innovation, or experimentation. Employees do what they are told without necessarily knowing why. There is no consultation, collaboration, or shared decision-making. As I mentioned earlier, this environment decreases job satisfaction, motivation, and engagement. The employee attrition rate increases, and attracting talent is challenging. The organization becomes inflexible and unable to adapt to a rapidly changing world. The leadership style is too rigid and fixed to adjust when needed.

Thankfully, this leadership style is disappearing – it's even less common in the military. In fact, one former military leader is actively championing the move away from command and control leadership. Retired four-star United States Army General Stanley McChrystal[80] led the US's premier military counter-terrorism force, the Joint Special Operations Command (JSOC). In 2011, he founded the McChrystal Group, which improves the performance of organizations and their leaders.

In his book *Team of Teams: New Rules of Engagement for a Complex World*, he says, "The temptation to lead as a chess master, controlling each move of the organization, must give way to an approach as a gardener, enabling rather than directing. A gardening approach to leadership is anything but passive. The leader acts as an "Eyes-On, Hands-Off" enabler who creates and maintains an ecosystem in which the organization operates."[81]

We need the same in our organizations, where employees are empowered rather than controlled. That's the focus of this final section.

Moving beyond command and control

The Empowerment and Trust Value Model illustrates what happens as leaders move from command and control.

Command and Control to Empowerment and Trust

Eminence Through Empowerment

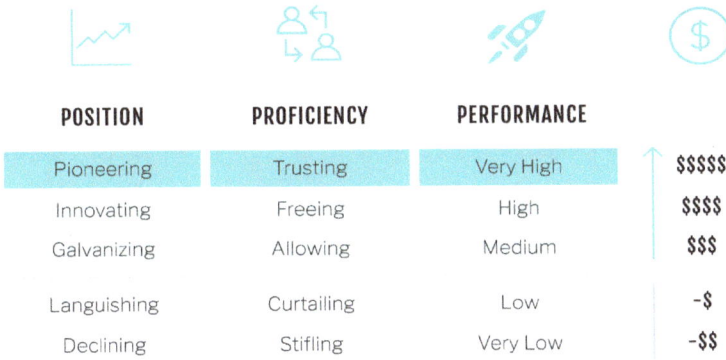

POSITION	PROFICIENCY	PERFORMANCE	
Pioneering	Trusting	Very High	$$$$$
Innovating	Freeing	High	$$$$
Galvanizing	Allowing	Medium	$$$
Languishing	Curtailing	Low	-$
Declining	Stifling	Very Low	-$$

Figure 29: The Empowerment and Trust Value Model

© 2024 Karen Ferris

While leaders continue to stifle and curtail employee capability with a command and control approach, organizations will languish and decline while their competition shines. In contrast, galvanizing the organization into action, driving innovation, and positioning it as a pioneer requires leaders to provide employees with autonomy, allowing them control over their work. When leaders give employees responsibility and decision-making rights, it results in trust-based relationships, ultimately increasing productivity, performance, and profitability.

I know many leaders are still at the command and control end of the leadership style spectrum because I work with them all the time. It is not that they do not want to move toward a more empowering leadership style; it is that they don't know where to start. In many cases, they have spent decades working with a particular leadership style, so the hard part of the learn-unlearn-relearn process is the *unlearn*.

They recognize that employees want autonomy, purpose, and meaningful work. They know that employees want ownership of their work and the ability to make decisions. However, when I run workshops with leadership teams and start talking about an empowerment and trust leadership style, I often see the "rabbit in the headlights" expression. Instead of hearing the word "trust," they hear the word "turmoil." For many, this is a massive mindset shift. So, where do you start?

Be transparent

First, you must be transparent about the change you will embark on. It is about having the courage to be vulnerable. It is about being brave, as we discussed earlier in the book. You must talk to your team and explain why you want to change your leadership style, what they will gain, and how you will approach it. You will garner trust when you demonstrate honesty and integrity, and your team will be more likely to support you and provide honest feedback.

You will ask for their understanding when you make mistakes or revert to your old leadership style. You must ask them to call it out when you do. Bring them along on your journey. They are your support team and cheerleaders. Be open to their feedback. Don't see the feedback as a threat, and don't take it personally. The feedback is about your leadership style, not about you as a person.

Start small and provide guardrails

One reason leaders I work with resist the unlearning and relearning process is that they see it as a massive undertaking. The enormity is overwhelming. The key is to start small. Start by delegating a small task you and your employee are comfortable with.

Another reason is the fear leaders have that something will go wrong while they are not directing the game of play. What if your employee makes a horrendous decision that costs the organization a lot of time and money to rectify?

Two things come into play regarding decision-making and risk. Firstly, start with something with minimal risk when delegating your first task. Not only will you feel more comfortable knowing that not much could go wrong, but so will your employees. The second thing is the provision of guardrails. These are parameters employees can operate within without seeking additional guidance or advice. Guardrails, like the protective barriers on the road, prevent or deter anyone from crossing into dangerous areas.

The guardrails you provide employees with should not be strict rules; they're merely boundaries. An employee can still decide to cross the boundary if they are comfortable making that decision. If you set hard and fast rules, you are reverting to command and control leadership. Use guardrails to empower decision-making.

The guardrails are not static. They are dynamic and will change over time as conditions and context change. You should formulate the guardrails with your team so they do not feel the guardrails are being enforced on them. Regularly review the guardrails with the team and determine if any amendments are needed.

Here are some examples of employee guardrails…

Let's say you're in sales and a customer asks for a discount on a service. You may have a guardrail that says you can apply a discount if it is twenty-five per cent or less. Above that, you should seek the advice of your manager. This is not a strict rule but a boundary to ensure that consideration is given to profitability and the customer's tenure.

If you're a content writer, your manager may tell you the ideal length for a press release is between 300 and 400 words. This is a guideline, not a rule. If you're struggling to keep the release under 450 words, you may want to consult your manager for advice or you may decide that those extra fifty words are needed.

If you're an IT system administrator, there may be a guardrail stating the optimum number of users on the system is 1,500, but you've just had a request to add fifty more new users. You have the independence to make the decision with the guardrail as your guidance. You know that performance could deteriorate if you add the new users, but you also know that system usage is low as it is the summer holidays. You can increase capacity to accommodate the new users and more before the end of the holidays. The impact will be negligible.

The Waterline Principle

Another way to provide guidance is to use the Waterline Principle, instituted by American engineer and entrepreneur Bill Gore, the co-founder of W.L. Gore & Associates, which makes innovative products such as Gore-Tex fabrics.[82]

Imagine your organization is a ship, and you are the captain. You can empower employees to make decisions if they shoot above the waterline. The decisions won't sink the ship, so the risk is minimal. If a decision should go awry and results in a hole in the side of the ship above the waterline, it can be fixed.

Figure 30: The waterline

If the decision is to shoot below the waterline, there is a higher risk to be considered, as it could blow a hole in the side of the ship below the waterline and sink the ship. Employees need to consider the risk if they are shooting below the waterline and may consider seeking guidance from the "captain" – you. You can then assess the risk and formulate the right decision.

If you are a business analyst proposing a major change to a key business process, you are shooting below the waterline. There is risk associated with the change, and so you will consult others about the proposal.

In contrast, let's say you're a facilities manager and the power has gone off in part of the building. You investigate and find the circuit breaker has tripped. There is only one switch flipped, which is for the lower floor. You decide to reset the switch.

You know that the lower floor has a plug load issue, which has been reported. As it is a known error with a workaround, you are shooting above the water line.

Get out of the way

An empowering mindset means you provide clarity of expectations, ensure understanding, provide the necessary support and resources, and then *get out of the way*. You must provide the space and opportunity for your employees to take ownership of, and be accountable for, delivering the specified outcomes. If they need any support and guidance, they can reach out to you.

When you do this, you become a respected leader. I created this model called "Let It Go" to illustrate the types of leadership that manifest as leaders move from command and control to empowerment and trust. There are two aspects at play. Leaders must surrender control and provide the employee with accountability for delivery. There is no place for micromanagement anymore. Leaders must also have a risk tolerance, but, as we have discussed, there are guardrails and waterlines in place to diminish the danger.

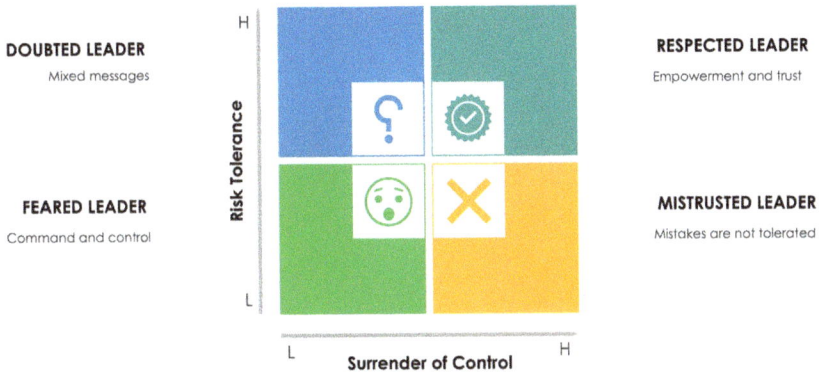

Figure 31: Let It Go Model

© 2024 Karen Ferris

At the bottom left is the command and control leader with no tolerance for risk while retaining total control. This is the *feared* leader. You must do as they say or suffer the consequences.

At the top left is the leader who is sending mixed messages. They display a risk appetite but will not surrender control. This is the *doubted* leader. They say they will tolerate risk but give employees no control over what they can do themselves.

The bottom right is the leader providing autonomy – surrendering control – but having no appetite for risk. The leader says, "You are on your own, Sunshine." This is the *mistrusted* leader. They say employees are empowered but will not tolerate any mistakes.

Top right is where you want to be – surrendering control and having a risk appetite. It is the leader with an empowering mindset. This is the *respected* leader.

Rinse and repeat

Each time you empower, trust, assign, and get out of the way, your comfort zone grows. After the first delegation, do it again. Pick a task that is a little more significant with maybe a little more risk. Do not overwhelm your employees – ensure they are comfortable with what is asked of them. It is okay to encourage and enable an employee to move into their stretch zone, but *do not* push them into the terror zone. It is where stress and anxiety occur, leading to burnout.

Figure 32: Comfort zone to terror zone

Chapter Brave introduced the concept of moving from the comfort zone into the stretch zone, along with this image, to illustrate that brave leaders know they must move into the stretch zone to grow. You also need to get comfortable with empowering your employees, which means getting into the stretch zone.

The more you empower your employees, the more time you will have to do what you should do as a leader. Your team will be more engaged, motivated, and productive. More creativity, innovation, and experimentation will lead you, the team, and the organization to success.

Note: I have interchangeably used the terms "delegation" and "empowerment." There is a real difference. As a leader, you can assign an employee a task, but you still need to empower them to undertake the task as they see best. You still need to provide them with the autonomy that comes with empowerment. When you assign a task, you must empower at the same time. Assigning a task without empowerment is demotivating.

Three leadership traits to instill psychological safety

You can truly empower your team if you create an environment of psychological safety.

In 1999, Harvard Professor Dr Amy Edmondson[83] studied medical teams and their number of mistakes. Her research did not return the results she expected. She found that the teams with the best outcomes also made the most mistakes. Further investigation revealed that the teams with good outcomes admitted to their mistakes while the others hid their mistakes.

She cemented the concept of psychological safety defined as, "The belief that one will not be punished or humiliated for speaking up with ideas, questions, concerns, or mistakes, and that the team is safe for interpersonal risk-taking."[84]

You cannot empower employees if you do not permit them to be their true selves. You and the team must be able to admit mistakes, challenge decisions, raise concerns, and ask questions. As I have stressed throughout this book, your team must feel they are in a psychologically safe work environment where they can contribute. It is an environment where they can take ownership, make decisions, and feel safe if mistakes happen.

In her book *The Fearless Organization*[85], Edmondson says there are three core leadership behaviors you must adopt to provide your team with psychological safety.

	SETTING THE STAGE	INVITING PARTICIPATION	RESPONDING PRODUCTIVELY
LEADERSHIP TASKS	**Frame the work** • Set expectations about failure, uncertainty, and interdependence to clarify the need for voice **Emphasize purpose** • Identify what's at stake, why it matters, and for whom it matters	**Demonstrate situational humility** • Acknowledge gaps **Practice inquiry** • Ask good questions • Model intense listening **Set up structures and processes** • Create forums for input • Provide guidelines for discussion	**Express appreciation** • Listen • Acknowledge and thank **Destigmatize failure** • Look forward • Offer help • Discuss, consider, and brainstorm next steps **Sanction clear violations**
ACCOMPLISHES	Shared expectations and meaning	Confidence that voice is welcome	Orientation toward continuous learning

Figure 33: Leadership tasks for psychological safety

Source: The Fearless Organization[86]

- **Setting the stage:** You must remind your team of their purpose and the importance of the work they do. Make it clear that there will be uncertainty and, as a result, there will be failures, which is okay. Embrace it. If we are not making mistakes, we are not progressing. We don't have to have all of the answers to a problem. When you normalize uncertainty, it makes it easier for everyone to talk about it. Tell everyone that you need their voice, whether that is calling out a concern or sharing an idea.

- **Inviting participation:** Invite engagement and ask questions. "What do you think?" "What are we missing?" Seek feedback and actively listen. Share information. Ways to invite participation and knowledge-sharing include focus groups, cross-functional teams charged with solving problems, peer-to-peer learning, digital suggestion boxes, and organizing meetings that have allocated time for everyone's input.

- **Responding productively:** When you ask someone a direct question, that person is then put on the spot and obliged to respond in a productive manner. When you have asked for feedback and received it, you do not have to agree with it, but you must be respectful and appreciative of the fact that it has been given. Say, "How can I help?" It is your job to empower everyone in your team by creating the conditions in which they can best contribute to the organization's goals.

Over two decades after the publication of Edmondson's research, a McKinsey article, titled "What is psychological safety?"[87] called out the lack of psychological safety in the workplace. The author said that despite the benefits of workplace psychological safety being well established since the research findings, it is not a given and is not the norm in most teams. The article states, "In fact, a McKinsey Global Survey[88] conducted during the pandemic indicated that the behaviors that create a psychologically safe environment are few and far between in leadership teams and organizations more broadly."

There is work to be done. You must be clear about what psychological safety is and is not. As already outlined, employees should feel safe to take interpersonal risks, speak up, disagree openly, raise concerns, give feedback, be vulnerable, and admit mistakes without fear of repercussions or reprisal.

It is not about being nice or mollycoddling, it is not an alternative word for "trust," it is not about blind tolerance of others, and it is not about removing accountability. It is not about wrapping people in bubble wrap and insulating them from threats and friction. It is not about overprotection. It is not about avoiding difficult conversations or avoiding conflict. On the contrary, psychological safety creates an environment where conflicting ideas and diverse perspectives are accepted and encouraged in a safe and respectful space.

Aligning the purpose

To truly empower your employees, they must have a sense of purpose aligned with the organizational purpose. Undertaking work that does not seem to have a purpose is both demotivating and demoralizing. Since the pandemic, employees have reconsidered what they want from their personal and professional lives. I call this The Great Reflection.

According to research conducted by McKinsey, seventy per cent of employees found their sense of purpose through their work.[89] The research also discovered that only eighteen per cent of respondents believed they get as much purpose from work as they want. Almost two-thirds (sixty-two per cent) said that while they get *some* purpose from work, they want to get even more. There was a significant impact on those who got some purpose but wanted more. They reported lower average work and life outcomes than their satisfied colleagues – from reduced energy and life satisfaction to lower engagement, satisfaction, and excitement about work. Negative work and life outcomes for employees will translate to negative outcomes for the business.

The starting point is to ensure the organization has a purpose behind which employees and customers can rally. It must be more than profit or market share. The World Economic Forum states, "The purpose of 'purpose' is both internal and external. Internally, purpose is a galvanizing force that unites employees and persuades them to work toward a common goal. And the goal should be such that it inspires pride in its employees."[90]

The organizational purpose could contribute to a more equitable world or increased sustainability. When organizations do this, the customer base will increase as consumers continue to demand more ethical and socially conscious businesses. In turn, profitability increases.

As a leader, you must make the organizational purpose visible to your employees. You must then link their jobs to that purpose and highlight how individuals across all functions and levels can fulfill that purpose. Walmart is a great example. It states, "We aim to build a better world – helping people live better and renew the planet while building thriving, resilient communities. For us, this means working to create opportunity, build a more sustainable future, advance diversity, equity, and inclusion, and bring communities closer together."[91]

Walmart upholds its commitments to opportunity; sustainability; community; ethics and integrity; culture, diversity, equity, and inclusion (CDE&I); philanthropy; environmental, social, and governance (ESG); and health and wellness in its everyday operations. It can link every one of its 2.3 million associates' roles to its purpose.

For example, for more than fifteen years, Walmart has been collaborating with other organizations to drive positive impact across global supply chains. Its focus on climate, nature, waste, and people in supply chains has strengthened the business and communities in measurable ways. Meanwhile, Walmart and the Walmart Foundation provide billions of dollars in cash and in-kind annual giving. Walmart focuses on areas where it can do the most good, combining its unique strengths with its philanthropy.

Aligning employees and teams behind an organizational purpose makes work matter. As a result, productivity, innovation, engagement, and retention increase. It gives employees a sense of pride in their work, increases motivation, and improves physical and mental well-being.

Setting the bar

As a leader, you will want to set the bar at the right height to get the best results from your team. If you set it too high, your team will be frustrated, demoralized, and demotivated as they fail to reach the bar. If you set it too low, you are saying that you do not expect much from your team, and you will get low results. People tend to aim at the target they have been given.

Find the level that will stretch the team but not overwhelm them so that it results in stress, anxiety, and burnout. It is your job to help everyone on the team reach the bar. Some will do it most of the time, and your job is to remove obstacles and provide resources as needed. Others may struggle, and your job is to coach and support those team members.

Make it known that experiencing setbacks is okay. If you are not experiencing setbacks, you are not moving forward. Setbacks are learning opportunities that take you a step closer to the bar. American basketball legend Michael Jordon famously said, "I've missed more than 9,000 shots in my career. I've lost almost 300 games. Twenty-six times, I've been trusted to take the game-winning shot and missed. I've failed over and over and over again in my life. And that is why I succeed."[92]

In an earlier section, I referred to Dr Carol Dweck in relation to the growth mindset. Dweck also talks about the power of "not yet." At a high school in Chicago, students must pass several courses to graduate. Instead of issuing a fail grade to those who do not pass, the school simply writes "Not yet" on the students' report cards. Two small yet extremely powerful words give students hope that if they keep trying, they will achieve a pass. You can use the same approach in the workplace, giving those striving to reach the bar the reassurance that they are on a learning curve and are not a failure.

A key thing to remember is that once you have set the bar, you do not want to lower it. If you lower it, you are sending a message that the team is not good enough, and, therefore, you will lower the bar to match their capability. You are telling them that they cannot live up to your expectations. It is demoralizing for everyone. So, it is important to set the bar at the right level and then raise it at the right time to get the team to perform at their best.

The power of recognition

One of the leadership tasks referred to earlier, in "Mindful," was expressing appreciation of others. You must listen, acknowledge, and thank. When you empower your employees, you must recognize them for their contributions.

Gallup and Workhuman surveyed over 13,000 adults employed full-time or part-time in twelve countries. The "Transforming Workplaces Through Recognition" report recognized that employers cannot just offer people jobs anymore. They must create an environment where employees want to work and can be their best. It starts with showing employees that they are valued. Reward and recognition achieve this.[93]

If organizations truly want to attract and retain talent for survival, they must demonstrate to employees that they are valued by recognizing their contributions. There is also a return on investment. Gallup reported that creating a culture of recognition can save a 10,000-employee company up to 16.1 million dollars in turnover costs annually.

While sixty-seven per cent of leaders and sixty-one per cent of managers say they give recognition a few times a week or more, forty per cent of employees report receiving recognition only a few times a year or less from a leader, manager, or supervisor.

When organizations do hit the mark, employees are:

- Seventy-three per cent less likely to "always" or "very often" feel burnt out
- Fifty-six per cent less likely to be looking or watching for job opportunities
- Forty-four per cent more likely to be "thriving" in their life overall

- Five times as likely to feel connected to their workplace culture
- Four times as likely to be engaged
- Five times as likely to see a path to grow at their organization
- Four times as likely to recommend the organization to friends or family

Recognizing employee efforts has clear benefits for the individual, team, and organization.

I realized the power of recognition early in my IT career. I took a position looking after a service desk supporting the internal business of a retail company. It didn't take long to realize there was work to be done. The service analysts were in the far left-hand corner of a massive open-plan expanse, which was warehouse-like. The rest of the space was occupied by programmers, analysts, system administrators, and technicians.

While getting to know the service analysts, it became clear that they had little self-esteem or self-confidence. They had been allocated the far-flung corner of the building, and, without it being voiced, they were covertly seen as the "failed programmers who now did support." There was no sense of "team." I put a few things in place, such as agreeing on the team's name so they could provide a consistent response when people called. Yes, that is how bad it was!

The service analysts had no headsets. They took calls with the phone handset under their chin while entering the call details into the computer. I told them that this was unacceptable for their role and that I would order headsets if they wanted them. I was telling them that I appreciated what they did and I would do what I could to make their job easier.

All the women were keen to get headsets, while the men said no, thinking it was not manly! I ordered enough headsets for everyone and handed the women theirs. It did not take long for the men with phone handsets under their chins to realize how much easier the job was with a headset. They sheepishly asked if they could also have headsets, and their request was instantaneously met as I opened my desk drawer.

That small gesture was the start of an increase in their self-esteem. They felt cared for, appreciated, and recognized. I also coached them in customer service, service management, and being value-driven. People utilizing the service desk also noticed an improvement. I started receiving phone calls and emails praising the service that the analysts had provided. Each time I received praise and positive feedback, I shared it with the individual, the rest of the team, and the wider IT cohort. They were receiving recognition.

There was one character on the service desk, who I shall call Robert, who was going to be a challenge. He wasn't going to change without some coercing. On one occasion, he answered the phone and said, "What the f*** are you calling me for?" He wasn't a bad employee, just a rogue who thought that opening line was funny.

He wanted to be liked, and, of course, all the other analysts were receiving recognition, praise, appreciation, and accolades because of the changes they had made. Positive peer pressure kicked in. Without Robert's colleagues explicitly asking him to change, the public recognition they were receiving influenced him to adapt his behavior and adopt the values they were exhibiting.

Then, one day, the service desk phone rang, and Robert answered it. "Hi, you have reached IT support – this is Robert.

How may I help you?" You could have heard a pin drop. Robert went on to be the greatest advocate for customer service, service management, and being value-driven. Recognition had lit a fire within him.

The power of recognition!

The five pillars of recognition

There are five pillars of recognition critical to driving its impact.

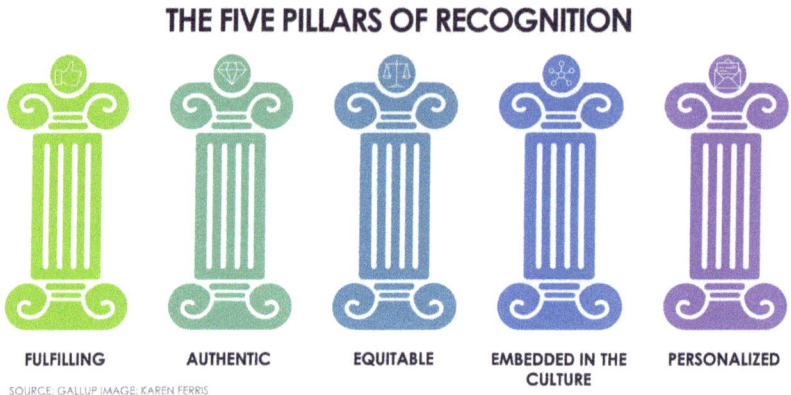

THE FIVE PILLARS OF RECOGNITION

| FULFILLING | AUTHENTIC | EQUITABLE | EMBEDDED IN THE CULTURE | PERSONALIZED |

SOURCE: GALLUP IMAGE: KAREN FERRIS

Figure 34: The five pillars of recognition

Fulfilling

The recognition must be fulfilling in that it must satisfy the needs of your employees. It must encourage and motivate. You recognize your employee's behavior when you want to see more of the same from them and others.

If you ask me, there is no right answer regarding how often you should give employee feedback. Every employee is different, and their needs vary. Your objective should be to create a consistent and reliable experience of being appreciated that makes employees feel valued and validates their efforts.

Based on my experience, I would recommend providing recognition a few times a month as the bare minimum, noting that recognition can be as simple as a verbal acknowledgment of an achievement. The recognition must also recognize the right behaviors at the right time and in the right way.

Positive reinforcement

I see recognition as the same as positive reinforcement. Behavioral psychologists use positive reinforcement to teach and strengthen behaviors. When someone exhibits a particular behavior, adding a reinforcing stimulus through positive reinforcement makes it more likely that they will repeat the same behavior in the future. A favorable outcome, event, or reward following an action strengthens the particular response or behavior.

As a leader, you can apply positive reinforcement when you observe or hear a member of your team displaying a behavior you would like to see more of. The behavior might be supporting a team member, innovating, problem-solving, using initiative, providing great customer service, or showing leadership capabilities.

Positive reinforcement will both acknowledge a desired behavior and encourage that behavior. You can provide positive reinforcement in many ways, including:

- Public recognition and praise
- Private recognition and praise
- Saying thank you
- Gift cards
- Concert or movie tickets
- Celebration breakfast/lunch/dinner
- Monetary rewards
- A physical or virtual pat on the back

Give positive reinforcement when the behavior occurs or as soon as possible afterward. Timely reinforcement results in more of the same behavior. The longer the gap, the less effective the reinforcement. Delaying reinforcement may reinforce the behavior occurring at the time of the reinforcement, not the behavior it should have reinforced.

If an employee complains about not being recognized and then receives a reward, you are reinforcing their complaining, not what they did to earn the reward. Reinforcement also loses value when delayed so long that employees find it difficult to remember the exact behavior they exhibited to earn the reward.

The reinforcement is only effective if you are clear about the behavior you are recognizing. A passing comment such as "Good job" provides the employee with no indication of what action or behavior is being praised. An employee can only repeat a behavior when you clarify that desired behavior. When you tell an employee, "That was a great proposal you presented to the board, and I appreciate the extra effort you put in to deliver it on time," the employee knows that you recognize the quality of the proposal, the presentation preparation, and the effort expended.

Make it special. People must earn positive reinforcement. There must be a direct link between the behavior exhibited and the reinforcer. Many of the benefits, rewards, and even compensation that employees receive often aren't for an accomplishment but for being in the right place at the right time. For example, a pay raise may be something everyone gets every year. The reinforcer must be something above and beyond what comes with the job. It must be unique and restricted to something "earned."

Authentic

In addition to the right amount of recognition, timing, and specificity, recognition must be authentic. Empty words and gestures undermine the experience and make it worthless. Whether recognition is delivered impersonally or unceremoniously as a matter of routine or obligation, or delivered in a personalized, genuine, and authentic way will make or break organizations reaping the benefits mentioned earlier.

I recommend recognizing achievements at least a few times a month, driven by factors beyond organizational targets. It is not a target or a KPI you must achieve. It must be recognition for achievements and contributions that make employees feel valued. Recognition must be genuine and appropriately given.

Equitable

Recognition not only impacts the recipient but also the perceptions of others. When employees perceive recognition to be out of balance – particularly when they feel overlooked – it triggers emotions of unfairness and exclusion, and adversely damages their employee experience.

A lack of equity sends messages about who is and who is not recognized in the organization. Recognition must give credit where credit is due, and a lack of perceived equity signals a severe failure. Two things are at play here – defining what warrants recognition and removing bias.

What warrants recognition?

If you recognize an employee for doing something expected of them, such as attending meetings on time, it destroys the validity of recognition. The organization must provide guidelines around what constitutes recognition. Note that I say "guidelines" and not "policy." There are many reasons for giving recognition. The existence of guidelines opens the door to having a corrective conversation when recognition is not delivered equitably.

Recognition should be given when an employee goes above and beyond their primary job responsibilities, which could include behaviors such as:

- Initiative and innovation
- Creative thinking
- Tenacity
- Supporting a colleague
- Resourcefulness
- Exemplifying organizational values
- Exceptional service to a customer or colleague
- Milestones such as tenure
- Specific achievement
- Raising team morale

These are just some ideas; collate your list based on the behaviors you wish to see more of. When you recognize a particular behavior or achievement, you are using positive reinforcement, which encourages the recipient and those around them to do more of the same.

Removal of bias

Recognition must be fair and equitable, meaning there is no place for bias. Your life experiences affect how you see the world, and that lens can create an unconscious bias you are not even aware of.

Something that happened in your life can trigger you to quickly judge others. It could be a protective pattern against danger. However, as we've already discussed, unconscious bias is extremely dangerous when you judge someone on personal characteristics they cannot change, such as their gender, race, ethnicity, sexual orientation, age, religion, and so on.

Another bias has entered the workplace as remote and hybrid working has become more commonplace: proximity bias. As you know from our discussion in "Mindful," proximity bias is an unconscious – and unwise – tendency to give preferential treatment to those in your immediate vicinity. While initially this was a matter of location within an office, it is now about those working in the office and those working remotely.

Here are some key steps to overcome proximity bias:

- **Increase awareness:** Make sure everyone is aware of the bias and the impact it can have. Acknowledge it as a potential issue.
- **Self-assess:** Continually assess yourself and your disposition to proximity bias. Are you giving preferential access to resources, information, or opportunities to those in your immediate vicinity?
- **Seek feedback from others:** Ask others to tell you if they think you are prone to proximity bias and in what context.
- **Look at the data:** Look at the assignments and opportunities you have given employees over a given period and whether it indicates any bias of allocation based on location.
- **Have a conversation:** Discuss diversity, equity, inclusion, and belonging in the workplace and how you can work to improve it.
- **Hold everyone accountable, including yourself:** Call it out when proximity bias is present and work to remove it.
- **Act:** Act on your findings. Deliverables, contribution, and value-add are more important than employee location.

Embedded in the culture

Recognition must be a way of life within the organization. It is not about having a recognition program. It is about a culture in which everyone can freely provide gratitude, praise, and appreciation to others.

When employees receive public recognition, it boosts the recognition culture. The organization must be prepared to demonstrate its culture of recognition – it must walk the talk. Recognition should be everyone's business. Everyone must be able to recognize anyone else in the organization. The recognition guidelines should indicate the sort of behaviors that constitute recognition.

Personalized

Personalize recognition. It must meet the needs of the recipient. Ask them how they would like to be recognized. Some people like being in the spotlight, but not everyone does.

There must be flexibility for you to personalize recognition and ensure it creates the intended impact. This means knowing the recipient and asking for their preferences. For example, do not give a vegetarian a coupon for a free meal at a steakhouse. Do not give an introvert the opportunity to appear center stage at the next company-wide gathering without checking in with them first.

Real-world example: Bay of Pigs

The 1961 Bay of Pigs fiasco is an example of people not feeling empowered and not being in an environment of psychological safety.

The mission was to take down Cuban revolutionary Fidel Castro and turn back communism. The plan was that 1,400 Cuban exiles stationed in Guatemala whom the CIA had trained would storm the beachhead at the Bay of Pigs, armed with American artillery, and march on Havana. The Cuban people would accordingly revolt against Castro, and then US President John Kennedy would bask in the glory of having turned back communism.

The air and naval resources to be made available were pulled at the last minute. The 1,400 Cuban exiles encountered a superior force of 20,000 Cuban soldiers and, without support from air or sea, they were either taken prisoner or killed. The whole thing was over in three days. Castro became a hero, and Kennedy was humiliated.

Kennedy said, "There were fifty or so of us, presumably the most experienced and smartest people we could get, but five minutes after it began to fall in, we all looked at each other and asked, 'How could we have been so stupid?'" The smartest people included Robert McNamara, Robert Kennedy, Arthur Schlesinger, Jr., Allen Dulles, and about forty others.

Although Kennedy's advisers had good reason to believe the mission would fail, they kept quiet. They did not want to be labeled "soft" or "cowardly" in the eyes of their colleagues. One of the advisers, Arthur Schlesinger, Jr., said Kennedy's "senior officials ... were unanimous for going ahead ... Had one senior adviser opposed the adventure, I believe Kennedy would have canceled it. No one spoke against it."[94]

There was a lack of empowerment and psychological safety that would have allowed one, if not more, advisers to speak up without fear of reprisal. Yale psychologist Irving Janis coined this behavior "groupthink."

Your REMARKABLE legacy

A few years ago, a friend of mine, Henry, approached me to act as both a coach and mentor to help him become a better leader. He had already embarked on the first step of the leadership journey – **separation** –following a wake-up call. He had asked for feedback from both colleagues and his team, and recognized that his current behaviors would hinder his success and that of his team. He understood the nature of the journey, including what was required, and started the **initiation** stage.

We mapped out his learning journey, identifying the skills and elements of the REMARKABLE leadership mindset he needed to develop or improve. Henry was already competent in some of the elements. We identified the priority elements to be learned, and, for each, we captured his goals, his approach, and his timeframe. We put aside the remaining elements, as they would be addressed in a subsequent learning journey.

Henry's initial focus was on the elements of empowering, listening, mindful, and accountable. He commenced his learning and put into practice the new skills. I was a member of his support team, helping him step outside of his comfort zone and into the learning zone. He used the guidance that I have now provided in this book to develop in each of his focus areas.

The initiation stage of Henry's journey took thirteen months. Despite this, he was motivated and energized to move into the **return** stage. He continued to apply his learning by doing, and soliciting feedback on his performance so he could adapt as needed.

Henry solicited feedback from the same colleagues and team members who had given him the initial feedback (which was his wake-up call). To say that the second round of feedback was tremendous is an understatement. It certainly exceeded Henry's expectations. It was like reading feedback on a totally different person who was now being described as an exceptional leader.

Henry was inspired and enthused to prepare for the next part of his learning journey.

The journey doesn't end here

As you turn the final page of this exploration into the REMARKABLE leadership mindset, you must recognize that the journey doesn't end here – it merely shifts to a new beginning. The principles and insights laid out in the preceding chapters are concepts to understand and actions to live by. As you've discovered, leadership is an ongoing process of learning, unlearning, and relearning. It is a dance with change, not a resistance to it.

As you move forward on your journey, here are the key points to keep in mind:

- In the face of constant disruption, leaders and individuals alike must be resilient, not just bouncing back from setbacks but bouncing forward, using challenges as catalysts for growth and innovation.

- Empathy must be the compass that guides your decision-making, ensuring that the mechanics of business never overshadow the humanity of your teams and the individuals within them.

- A mindful mindset enables you to be present, in the moment, calm, self-aware, compassionate, and accepting without judgment. This will reduce anxiety and stress, increase focus and attention, improve relationships, and elevate creativity.

- As an adaptive leader, you can lead with the courage and skill to challenge the status quo, deploy yourself with agility, and mobilize others to step into the unknown. You can stay ahead of the game and inspire your team.

- A resourceful mindset will enable you to find efficient and innovative ways to overcome problems and challenges. You will do whatever it takes to complete the job with what you have available. You will be persistent, open-minded, and prepared to change your approach when needed.

- You can make yourself **known** – for the right reasons and to the right people – by building your leadership brand. This means telling people who you are, what your values and beliefs are, and the worth you bring.

- Your ability to build a culture of **accountability** will drive organizational success through increased employee engagement and motivation.

- Being courageous is core to outstanding leadership, and you are now equipped to be a **brave** leader. You are prepared to be vulnerable, embrace setbacks as learning opportunities, break the rules for the betterment of everyone, have hard conversations, and make hard decisions.

- A **listening** mindset allows you to truly listen to, empathize with, and better understand other people. It enables you to be present, attentive, and non-judgmental. In addition, being intentional about your communication helps you analyze different audiences and be empathetic about their needs.

- You can **empower** your employees by giving them the autonomy to make their own decisions and own their work. You provide the tools, resources, and support needed. This increases employee engagement, creativity, innovation, and motivation.

As we adapt to an evolving workplace shaped by AI, global crises, and the ever-accelerating pace of change, the REMARKABLE mindset is your key to unlocking potential – both within yourself and those you lead.

Take these principles. Apply them with courage and consistency. Become the leader who doesn't just survive the tumultuous tides of change but thrives within them, setting a standard for what it means to be truly REMARKABLE. And remember, the world is not waiting for leaders who will merely fill the shoes of those who came before but for those who will dare to walk new paths and leave footprints worth following.

Thank you for joining me on this journey. The future is unwritten, and the pen is in your hands. What will you write?

Endnotes

1. https://en.wikipedia.org/wiki/Future_Shock

2. https://www.amazon.com/What-Got-Here-Wont-There/dp/1846681375

3. https://twitter.com/AdamMGrant/status/1437408114899357699?lang=en

4. https://en.wikipedia.org/wiki/The_Hero_with_a_Thousand_Faces

5. https://www.drphil.com/advice/dr-phils-ten-life-laws

6. https://www.apa.org/topics/resilience

7. https://www.amazon.com/Unleash-Resiliator-Within-Resilience-Individuals/dp/0648469433

8. https://en.wikipedia.org/wiki/Emotional_Intelligence

9. https://www.ey.com/en_us/news/2023/03/new-ey-us-consulting-study

10. http://www.creativeeducationfoundation.org/creative-problem-solving/the-cps-process/

11. The CPS Learners Model comprises the work of G.J. Puccio, M. Mance, M.C. Murdock, B. Miller, J. Vehar, R. Firestien, S. Thurber, & D. Nielsen.

12. https://dschool.stanford.edu/

13. https://en.wikipedia.org/wiki/Albert_Bandura

14. https://en.wikipedia.org/wiki/Self-efficacy

15. https://www.researchgate.net/publication/226807199_Expectation_fantasy_and_weight_loss_Is_the_impact_of_positive_thinking_always_positive

16. https://journals.aom.org/doi/abs/10.5465/amr.2001.4378011

17. https://en.wikipedia.org/wiki/Thomas_Edison

18. https://www.forbes.com/sites/daviddisalvo/2017/06/05/six-science-based-reasons-why-laughter-is-the-best-medicine/#614e8bd67f04

19. https://en.wikipedia.org/wiki/Robert_A._Emmons

20. https://en.wikipedia.org/wiki/Thomas_J._Watson

21. https://www.amazon.com/Unleash-Resiliator-Within-Resilience-Handbook-ebook/dp/B089GK6R7W

22. https://en.wikipedia.org/wiki/Warren_Bennis

23. https://www.azquotes.com/author/26340-Arie_de_Geus

24. https://www.abrahamlincolnonline.org/lincoln/education/failures.htm

25. https://www.catalyst.org/reports/empathy-work-strategy-crisis

26. https://newground.org/about/our-founders-vision/

27. https://newground.org/get-inspired/

28. https://en.wikipedia.org/wiki/Cognitive_behavioral_therapy

29. https://www.businessolver.com/news/businessolver-study-reveals-decline-in-workplace-empathy/

30. https://www.businessolver.com/news/businessolver-study-reveals-decline-in-workplace-empathy/

31. https://www.who.int/southeastasia/health-topics/mental-health/key-terms-and-definitions-in-mental-health#stigma

32. https://diversio.com/empathetic-leadership-supports-diverse-equitable-workforces/

33. https://www.mindful.org/what-is-mindfulness/

34. https://books.google.com.au/books/about/A_Theory_of_Objective_Self_Awareness.html?id=zhF-AAAAMAAJ&redir_esc=y

35. https://hbr.org/2018/01/what-self-awareness-really-is-and-how-to-cultivate-it

36. https://hbr.org/2018/01/what-self-awareness-really-is-and-how-to-cultivate-it

37. https://journals.sagepub.com/doi/
abs/10.1177/0149206315604187?mod=article_inline&

38. https://www.sog.unc.edu/sites/www.sog.unc.edu/files/course_
materials/Cognitive%20Biases%20Codex.pdf

39. https://www.unispace.com/news/workplace-insights-report-
global-press

40. https://hrexecutive.com/proximity-bias-a-likely-reality-say-most-
leaders/

41. https://en.wikipedia.org/wiki/Mahatma_Gandhi

42. https://www.ncronline.org/blogs/francis-chronicles/popes-
quotes-bishops-mission

43. https://a.co/d/ast9kuW

44. https://en.wikipedia.org/wiki/Carol_Dweck

45. https://www.amazon.com/Mindset-Psychology-Carol-S-Dweck/
dp/0345472322

46. https://a.co/d/gaVcg1B

47. https://a.co/d/gaVcg1B

48. http://smgrp.com.au/wp-content/uploads/2016/09/The-Work-of-
Leadership-Heifetz.pdf

49. https://en.wikipedia.org/wiki/Dwight_D._Eisenhower

50. https://www.goodreads.com/quotes/6371-those-who-cannot-
change-their-minds-cannot-change-anything

51. https://en.wikipedia.org/wiki/Steve_Jobs

52. https://en.wikipedia.org/wiki/Steve_Wozniak

53. https://www.linkedin.com/pulse/trust-matrix-richard-barrett/

54. https://brenebrown.com/

55. https://garyvaynerchuk.com/

56. https://tim.blog/

57. https://www.gilderlehrman.org/about/bruce-gordon

58. https://www.warren.af.mil/News/Commentaries/Article/636097/
president-trumans-leadership-lessons-inspire-leaders-today/

59. https://en.wikipedia.org/wiki/Satya_Nadella

60. https://www.geekwire.com/2020/uncharted-territory-read-satya-nadellas-email-microsoft-employees-covid-19-outbreak/

61. https://en.wikipedia.org/wiki/Howard_Schultz

62. https://www.forbes.com/sites/clareoconnor/2013/12/04/starbucks-billionaire-howard-schultz-to-oprah-its-ok-for-men-to-cry-even-ceos/?sh=6d36f2ab3d7a

63. http://intelligentdisobedience.com/books/

64. https://www.afr.com/work-and-careers/management/why-the-best-leaders-separate-difficult-decisions-from-unpleasant-ones-20230411-p5czk7

65. https://www.ddiworld.com/global-leadership-forecast-2023

66. https://en.wikipedia.org/wiki/Malala_Yousafzai

67. https://malala.org/newsroom/malala-nobel-speech

68. https://a.co/d/cUHPZxL

69. https://en.wikipedia.org/wiki/Dale_Carnegie

70. https://www.penguinrandomhouse.ca/books/85559/dialogue-by-william-isaacs/9780385479998/excerpt

71. https://www.miklagardarts.com/theodore-zeldins-muse-conversations

72. https://journals.aom.org/doi/abs/10.5465/amj.2021.0245

73. https://www.theceomagazine.com/business/management-leadership/the-single-biggest-problem-with-communication/

74. https://en.wikipedia.org/wiki/IKEA

75. https://www.npr.org/2020/01/07/794281632/ikea-reaches-46-million-settlement-over-death-of-toddler-killed-by-dresser-tip-o

76. https://en.wikipedia.org/wiki/The_7_Habits_of_Highly_Effective_People

77. https://pubmed.ncbi.nlm.nih.gov/6486600/

78. https://en.wikipedia.org/wiki/Titanic

79. https://psycnet.apa.org/doiLanding?doi=10.1037%2Fa0022676

80. https://en.wikipedia.org/wiki/Stanley_A._McChrystal

81. https://www.goodreads.com/author/quotes/3898235.Stanley_McChrystal

82. https://www.gore.com/about/the-gore-story#our-culture

83. https://en.wikipedia.org/wiki/Amy_Edmondson

84. https://amycedmondson.com/psychological-safety/

85. https://www.amazon.com/Fearless-Organization-Psychological-Workplace-Innovation/dp/1119477247

86. https://www.strategy-business.com/article/How-Fearless-Organizations-Succeed

87. https://www.mckinsey.com/featured-insights/mckinsey-explainers/what-is-psychological-safety

88. https://www.mckinsey.com/capabilities/people-and-organizational-performance/our-insights/psychological-safety-and-the-critical-role-of-leadership-development

89. https://www.mckinsey.com/capabilities/people-and-organizational-performance/our-insights/help-your-employees-find-purpose-or-watch-them-leave

90. https://www.weforum.org/agenda/2023/01/purpose-essential-businesses-today-davos2023/

91. https://corporate.walmart.com/purpose#:~:text=We%20aim%20to%20build%20a,and%20bring%20communities%20closer%20together.

92. https://www.youtube.com/watch?v=4C_RVq-GrfU

93. https://www.workhuman.com/resources/reports-guides/unleashing-the-human-element-at-work-transforming-workplaces-through-recognition

94. https://neuroleadership.com/your-brain-at-work/jfk-inspired-term-groupthink/

www.ingramcontent.com/pod-product-compliance
Lightning Source LLC
Chambersburg PA
CBHW040753220326
41597CB00029BA/4753